A Columbia River Reader

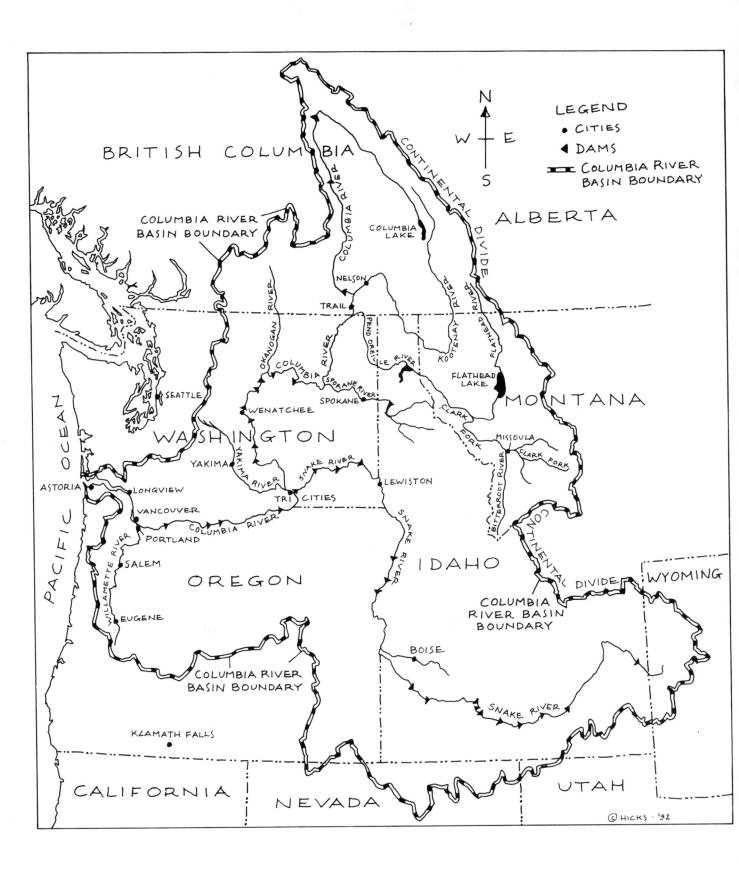

A Columbia River Reader

Edited by William L. Lang

Passage of The Dalles, 1867

The Center for Columbia River History,
a branch of the Washington State Historical Society
1992

Grateful acknowledgement is made to the following for permission to reprint the articles in *A Columbia River Reader*:

COLUMBIA

The Magazine of Northwest History

The Washington State Historical Society and *Columbia, the Magazine of Northwest History*, for permission to reprint "Riverworlds: The Sweep of Cultures and the Columbia," by James P. Ronda, in *Columbia*, vol. 5 (Fall 1991), pages 28-33; "Encounter on the Columbia: An Inner History of Trade and Its Consequences," by William L. Lang, in *Columbia*, vol. 6 (Summer 1992), pages 4-9; from "The Columbia Before It Was Tamed: How a Raging River Was Opened to Steamboat Traffic," by William D. Layman, in *Columbia*, vol. 1 (Winter 1988), pages 32-41; from "The Mystique of Grand Coulee Dam and the Reality of the Columbia Basin Project," by Paul C. Pitzer, in *Columbia*, vol. 4 (Summer 1990), pages 28-33; from "Longview: The Career of a Washington Model City," by Carl Abbott, in *Columbia*, vol. 4 (Summer 1990), pages 14-20; from "Historical Access to the Hanford Record: Problems in Investigating the Past," by Michele A. Stenehjem, in *Columbia*, vol. 3 (Winter 1989-90), pages 29-35.

Pacific Northwest Quarterly

The University of Washington and *Pacific Northwest Quarterly* for permission to reprint from "Wheat Sacks Out to Sea: The Early Export Trade from the Walla Walla Country," by Donald W. Meinig, in *Pacific Northwest Quarterly*, vol. 45 (January 1954), pages 13-18; "The New Settlers on the Yakima Project, 1880-1910," by C. Brewster Coulter, in *Pacific Northwest Quarterly*, vol. 61 (January 1970), pages 10-21; "The Coon-Neuberger Debates of 1955: `Ten Dam Nights in Oregon'," in *Pacific Northwest Quarterly*, vol. 55 (April 1964), pages 55-66.

OREGON Historical *Quarterly*

The Oregon Historical Society for permission to reprint from "The Women of Fort Vancouver," by John A. Hussey, in *Oregon Historical Quarterly*, vol. 92 (Fall 1991), pages 265-308; "Engineering the Cascades Canal and Locks, 1876-1896," by William F. Willingham, in *Oregon Historical Quarterly*, vol. 88 (Fall 1987), pages 229-55.

The University of Washington Press for permission to reprint from "Tales of Coyote: Eastern Washington Traditions," as told by Martin Louie, Sr., pages 164-9, and "Native Place Names on the Columbia Plateau," by Eugene S. Hunn, pages 170-7, in *A Time of Gathering: Native Heritage in Washington State*, edited by Robin K. Wright. Copyright 1991 by the University of Washington Press and the Thomas Burke Memorial Washington State Museum.

A Columbia River Reader is part of the Great River of the West project, a program of the Center for Columbia River History, funded by a major grant from the National Endowment for the Humanities with support from the Washington State Historical Society and Washington State University at Vancouver.

Center for Columbia River History, Washington State University-Vancouver, 1812 East McLoughlin Blvd., Vancouver, Washington 98663

Cover illustration by Evelyn Hicks. Photograph of The Dalles on the title page is used with the permission of the Oregon Historical Society, O.H. 21583, #1100-A.

We rivers, we torrents
We heavy-backed waters
Burned out of the green ocean,
Came, clouds, from the plunging
Sea restless as flame.
           – H. L. Davis, "Rivers to Children," 1928

Contents

Preface

Two centuries ago, American sea captain Robert Gray brought his ship, *Columbia Rediviva*, across a white-foamed breaker line at the mouth of a large river emptying into the Pacific Ocean. Gray named the river after his vessel and sketched the river's outlines on the first nautical chart to accurately depict the Columbia. Within months, British explorers had gone upriver more than a hundred miles and produced an even more detailed map of the river. From that time on, the river became known to the world beyond the Pacific Northwest.

The Columbia had existed as an idea and as an image long before its description by Gray, first as part of an imaginary geography that identified it as the Northwest Passage through the continent and later as a river carrying many names but always understood as the Great River of the West. But the reality of the river is much older than the hopeful geography inscribed by European cartographers. The natural history of the Columbia extends into geologically measured time, beyond human memory and awareness. It was born of fire and ice and was contorted into its modern course by explosive volcanic events and catastrophic floods. The last of these cataclysms carved the scablands of eastern Washington and the deep gorges of the middle river no more than 15,000 years ago. People have lived along the river and its tributaries for at least 11,000 years.

The great river has nurtured human communities for thousands of years, and it is the history of the relationships between the river and its people—from the earliest times to the present—that is the focus of this book and its sponsoring program, The Great River of the West: The Columbia River in Pacific Northwest History. In a series of public conferences and forums during 1992 and 1993, the Center for Columbia River History will introduce citizens of the region to the fascinating and centrally important history of our Great River of the West. The programs are designed to present to a broad public a range of the best and most comprehensive historical studies on the Columbia. The discussions generated by these presentations and the community forums using this book will aid the public in understanding the extended histories of important contemporary Columbia River issues. To accomplish this, the Center for Columbia River History received a generous grant from the National Endowment for the Humanities, with additional support from the Washington State Historical Society and Washington State University-Vancouver.

Our subject is vast, and its web of connections and consequences is intricate and complex. Any brief view of the Columbia's history is ultimately simplistic and distorting, but a truly "complete" history is beyond our grasp and threatens to bury us in unrelenting detail that ultimately confuses us. To begin with, the Columbia's dimensions are daunting and its statistics challenge us to find appropriate superlatives. It is a long and powerful river, extending more than 1,200 miles from its origins in the Canadian Rockies to its Pacific Ocean mouth and falling more than one foot per mile in its course to the sea. It ranks as the second largest river in volume in North America and fourth in length. The Columbia's modern flood of record in 1894 inundated downtown Portland with six feet of water. Its waters have nourished anadromous fish populations that have annually numbered in the millions.

Awesome as the Columbia's physical dimensions are, our curiosity is driven even harder by questions about how people have lived with the river, what they have thought about it, how they have used it, what it has meant to them. We should begin with these large questions, narrow our focus to smaller pieces of our history, and pursue them all with the specific histories our Columbia River communities have created. The bicentennial commemoration of Gray's entrance into the river is a great opportunity to engage in this pursuit, and these forum meetings offer an equally great opportunity to explore the links between our heritage and Columbia River issues that concern us today.

This book is meant as a suggestive text and resource to stimulate these public discussions. The articles included in it, some of which have been excerpted to condense their length, range from broad overviews of large topics to case studies of singular events and developments in Columbia River history. They were all published in regional journals or books during the last three decades, and some present the results of very recent research. In each, the authors offer their own distinct viewpoints on our shared past.

A Columbia River Reader is divided into two chronological sections, the first covering the pre-industrial history of the Columbia, the second dealing with events and developments since the 1880s. The first section considers Native American culture, the encounter between whites and Indians, and the uses Indians and invading whites made of the Columbia. In the second section, authors describe a new Columbia River environment that resulted from humans trying to manipulate the river and bending it to expanded uses, from navigation to nuclear engineering.

Each article focuses on one subject or event, but includes information on dozens of ancillary topics. The description of women's lives at Fort Vancouver during the early nineteenth century, for example, takes us inside the mechanics of the Hudson's Bay Company fur trade. Articles on Walla Walla's wheat trade and the river and the development of Longview, Washington, emphasize that Columbia River communities have lived by the cycles of the region's natural resource economy. Essays on Native American place names and the significance of Grand Coulee Dam point up how different the Columbia looks when seen through different lenses.

In all these essays, we learn that history is a seamless garment composed of many fibers, each connected and intertwined in endlessly fascinating and revealing patterns. The unifying chord of this region's history is the Columbia River; and as questions are asked about its past, we learn about the context of our lives. We are all people of Nch'i Wana, the Big River, and in studying it we study ourselves.

Acknowledgements

This book is part of a larger program initiated by the Washington State Historical Society in 1990. David Nicandri, Director of WSHS, had the foresight to establish the Center for Columbia River History as the Society's first branch operation, locating it at Washington State University-Vancouver. Dr. Hal Dengerink, WSU-Vancouver Campus Dean, supported the effort and welcomed the Center to his campus as a partner in the enterprise.

The Great River of the West Project is funded by the National Endowment for the Humanities. The project began with a major conference on the Columbia River in May 1992 in Vancouver, Washington. A conference series, beginning in May and concluding in October 1992, brought scholars to Columbia River communities to discuss the history of the river at the Yakima Heritage Museum in Yakima, the North Central Washington Museum in Wenatchee; the East Benton County and Franklin County museums in the Tri-Cities, Maryhill Museum in Goldendale, the Columbia River Maritime Museum in Astoria, Whitman College in Walla Walla, the Columbia River Gorge Discovery Center in The Dalles, and the Cowlitz County Museum in Kelso.

This book will be used in library/community forums in public libraries in the following Columbia River Basin cities: Lewiston, Idaho; Toppenish, Ilwaco, Omak, Kettle Falls, Ellensburg, and Camas, Washington; and Hood River and Hermiston, Oregon. David Nicandri, Dr. Robert Carriker, Dr. Eckard Toy, Dr. William L. Lang, and Laurie Mercier will lead the community discussions in these cities. Jennifer Jeffries Thompson conceived the library/community forum program and has contributed significantly to the entire Great River of the West project.

It is because of the efforts of regional historians and the cooperation of institutions, including the Columbia Arts Center of Vancouver, Washington, the Washington Commission for the Humanities, and Washington State University, that this program and book are possible. Editors of *Columbia, Pacific Northwest Quarterly, Oregon Historical Quarterly*, and the University of Washington Press graciously permitted the reprinting of materials that originally appeared in their publications.

This book was designed and composed by Marianne Keddington. Evelyn Hicks prepared the map and created the image on the cover. Additional help came from Garry Schalliol, Leslie Waltz, and Rebecca Lang. The National Endowment for the Humanities provided the funds to produce this volume, which is for use in Great River of the West programs and for free distribution to libraries.

Part I
The Natural River

Indian fishing platforms at Celilo Falls in about 1953
(Photo courtesy of the Oregon Historical Society, O.H. 76045)

Tales of Coyote
Eastern Washington Traditions
as told by Martin Louie, Sr.

These stories were recorded by Martin Louie, Sr., during January of 1988. They provide a sample of the many Plateau traditions involving the important mythical trickster/creator, Coyote. Coyote is important as a benefactor who transformed the world into its present state, but there are many sides to his character. In addition to his creative contributions, he is frequently shown to be greedy, deceitful, or obscene. In these stories, one of Coyote's most important contributions is described: bringing salmon up the rivers to the Plateau people..

Martin Louie, Sr., also known as Snpaḵtsín First Light in the Morning, is an elder of the Colville Confederated Tribes. He was born in 1906 and grew up in the Colville tradition, fishing, hunting, and gathering plants. He has exten-sive knowledge of eastern Washington traditions, and through the years has shared his expertise with many people. . . .

The people of the Plateau take sweat baths in small private structures built with willow frames. Rocks are heated in a fire outside the structure and brought inside with tongs. When water is sprinkled on the hot rocks, their intense heat transforms the water into a pore-penetrating mist. On the Plateau, Sweatlodge, or Q'uil sten, is believed to be a spiritual gift to be used for healing, prayer, meditation, and spiritual growth. For some, the construction of Sweatlodge is a sacred process, filled with symbolism. Each of the willows used is important, and together they represent the major elements of life on this planet: earth, water, sun, and air.

How the Sweathouse Was Made
1. The People Need Fish

In a time before humans, there were plant people and animal people. The animal people were at Kettle Falls, and they had only scrub fish. They couldn't get any salmon because there was a weir across the river, the Columbia River, down at Celilo. What is known as Warm Springs, Oregon, now. There were four women there that controlled the salmon, controlled the river: Seagull, and Snipe, Kill-deer, and Kingfish. Four ladies. And the chiefs, the chiefs called a meeting at the Council Tipi.

And there were four chiefs. The first, the leader, was Mr. Bear. The second chief was Cougar. The third chief, Bald Eagle. And the fourth chief was Salmon. All the people were there and they wanted some better fish. They wanted to select somebody wise who could get the salmon.

And Coyote, he was tricky. Nobody liked him. So they didn't invite him to this meeting at Kettle Falls. He went anyway, and he lay outside of the tipi and listened. The chief said, "We have to select somebody brave, somebody with power. There's people to be descended here, on earth, the human beings. They have to have fish. They have to have better fish than what we have now." So, Coyote listened and the chief said, "Well," he said, "not only that, but the human beings have to have a medicine house, a sweat lodge, to clean their bodies, their souls, their luck if

3

they're in a bad luck streak. They have to have somewhere to go pray to the earth, pray to the Creator."

So, Coyote got through listening. He thought, "I'm the man. I'll go down." And Coyote had power. So he went, on the east side of the Columbia River, all the way down and he got to thinking. Around Davenport or Wilbur, he got on the prairie. He went south and he kept thinking, "I wonder what the chief meant by `medicine house for the coming people'?"

When he had gone as far as Soap Lake he thought, "Well, maybe I've got it." So there was a patch of brush—willows—there. So he started cutting.

First he cut four poles and erected them for the four directions: east, north, west, and south. That's the four directions. So he cut four more and he erected them to make the sweathouse. That's the four seasons. That's winter spring, summer, and autumn. That's the four seasons. Then he thought . . . sat there for a while and he thought, "Now what?"

So he thought about the four foods. So he erected four more sticks for the sweathouse: bitterroots, serviceberries, salmon, and meat. That's the four foods. Now, the four colors: the east is yellow; the north is white; the west is black, that's the resting time; and, the south is green. Now he erected four more sticks: the four winds. The north wind, the west wind, south wind, eastern wind. That's the four winds. Now, the four nations. He thought, "Can't be just one nation. It's got to be four. So, the four nations: America, Europe, China, and Japan. Now, the four moons: the new moon, first quarter, full moon, last quarter.

And one stick he cut, put it around the bottom of the sweathouse. That one stick, clear around, means the world, clear around. Now, the major things of this earth are the earth, water, sun, and air. All these elements compose the Indian Sweatlodge.

2. Coyote Brings Out the Salmon

So Coyote went down from that sweat lodge. He went down. He got close to Celilo Falls and he wondered. "Those women are awful sharp-eyed and they're awful smart. How am I going to get there to break that weir and bring the salmon out?" So, he transformed himself into a little baby. He got a piece of bark and he lay on there and he started floating towards the falls. And the four women were there, guarding the falls. They heard a baby cry. They looked around; they saw that piece of bark floating down towards the falls. One of them jumped in, got the bark and the baby, brought it over . . . a little tiny baby. The oldest one didn't like it. "Somebody must be trying to get our salmon. The other three outvoted her. They took the little baby back.

These women, every morning they'd go dig roots, pick berries, get ready for the winter. They'd all go and they tied this little baby for safety, inside. When they left, Coyote untied himself and he ran to the falls where they had the salmon stopped. And, he looked it over. Finally he found a way. He thought, "Well, I can dig a channel around this over here and break that dam. The salmon, I can bring them up." So, before the ladies came back to the tipi, he went back and tied himself and put dirt on his face. He looked like he had been playing around in there.

Finally, on the fourth day, he had the dam pretty near broken. He took a ladle, soup ladle, made out of a buckhorn sheep horn. He put that on his head. And he thought, "If those women catch me on my last job, they can't brain me. They can club me but I won't feel it." So he put this ladle on his head and he went over there and he started digging again. He wasn't quite through—the water was just seeping through and the salmon were all behind him.

So, the ladies got back and there was no baby there. The oldest one said, "I told you! Let's run for the weir." They went down there and Coyote was just about to dig through. It was already seeping. They started pounding him on his head. And, they couldn't hurt him because of the ladle he had on his head. Finally, he broke through and he started running up the east side of the Columbia River. Told the salmon to follow him. So, they followed.

The first river he came to was on the west side of the Columbia. And that river is called the Yakima River. So he took the salmon up there and he traded for a young woman. So her people got salmon. When he left from there he came up the river a ways and he came to a place they call Entiat, or Nt'iyátkw. He traded some salmon there for another woman. Then he left from there. And he came to the Wenatchee River. . . . He traded some salmon there for another woman. He left from there. And, he came to Okanogan, mouth of Okanogan. He took the salmon up, all the way up, to Okanogan Falls and he put a dam in there, where the people could fish. He traded the salmon there. Then he went north from there. Went over the hill and he sat there. He was looking north. He was looking at Penticton, or Snpintktn. They sent a crippled woman over to trade for salmon. Coyote got embarrassed. He didn't want her. He said, "You people will have little bitty salmon." So, he took the fins off the salmon, threw them up the river. And that's how those Kickinees got up there. They are the fins off of the big salmon.

So, from there he came back down. Then he went up the Spokane River. He went up all the rivers. He traded for everything: food, medicine, everything. Then he went back to his sweat lodge at Soap Lake. When he got there, he distributed the food, the medicine, everything. And, he told the people, he said, "In due time, when the people are descended here, the human beings, that'll be their hospital. They'll call it Medicine House. Anybody—the sick, gamblers, Indian Doctors, Medicine People—all classes of people, will go over there and get rid of their stress, their bad luck."

And the last time that I know of, people used to go over there and have a ceremony—a ceremony there for one day. They'd leave some food—meat or fish—for Coyote. And the Chief would face four directions and turn, turn to his left. First, he faced to where the sun comes up and he turned the way the world turns. That's what they call Creator: the sun; it brings the warmth; the berries will berry; the little birds, the little animals will grow; and the fruit, roots, and everything will grow. They used to say that the east brings the happiness. Then he faced the north. The north changes the world. In the winter the snow comes, covers the land. When it breaks in the spring, the mountains and the hills will gather all deteriorated stuff and bring it down to the Columbia, the main channel, and take it away. The water gathers all deteriorated stuff and takes it south, piles it up on each side of the shore and what goes out on the ocean will never return. And we have a brand new world in spring. The high waters take everything out, wash everything down. That's why we pray to the water, every morning and night. You talk to everything.

Everything has to be alive on this earth. Everything is alive. And, if it wasn't for Mother Earth, we wouldn't be alive. If it wasn't for Father Water, nothing would live. Water holds everything's life on this world: the grass, the trees, the fruit, the animals, the birds, the human beings, everything. It wasn't for water, I guess we'd never survive. We'd turn into rock or something. . . . Then the leader turned to the west. That's when everybody is supposed to rest. You become a new man, a new woman, in the morning. He turned to the south at last. That's where all the good comes from. The animals, the birds that leave for the south return, the fruit will come, the roots will grow, and the salmon will return.

3. Coyote Makes Fish Traps

Well, Coyote got back from bringing the salmon up the Spokane River as far as Little Falls. Then he came up, gave salmon to all these creeks, Hall Creek and Barnaby Creek. He brought salmon to the Colville River, then he went on back to Kettle Falls.

There he told the people, "Now," he said, "we'll have to figure out what the coming people will use to catch the fish when they are descended here." He started by making traps (tselí?, J-shaped basketry traps) on the Colville River. He made some at Skwekwán't, "little waterfall" (Meyers Falls), way up the river. Then he made some at Kettle Falls. Everywhere he'd hang the fish trap, he'd name the place. At Kettle Falls, the first fish trap was hung at the place they call N?aw?áwyakn, "hanging upside down." That's on the east side of the river. The next one, hung on the east side, they call Skt'ak', "crossing."

Then he made a scaffold and spear points. He made a pole; made a spear. And he said, "That's what the coming people will use." He named all the places. Then he told his daughter, "In between Skt'ak' and Snk'eplanw'íxwtn, `cut-line-deliberately-place', sit in the middle of the river. Face downstream. The coming people will fish there, spear salmon. Hang your traps there." That's the one called Ki?antsútn, "keep-things-to-oneself-place."

He made a scaffold for harpooning salmon on the west side, calling it Weyí?stn, "fallen-vegetation-place." Then he named another place that had a swift ripple, a point. They call that Nkwu?t, "back eddy." Then he made a place where the people could cross on the canoe. They call that the crossing, St'at'ak'mtn, "crossing place." This is still a place of crossing. Now both bridges are there: the highway bridge and the railroad bridge cross at St'at'ak'mtn, and land on the east side.

He made a channel on the east side for the people from up north. That is now known as Hayes Island. Tkwumáks, "long point," is the name of the camping spot of the original Kettle Falls people. Nmxiynm, "having a grove of cedar trees," they spear salmon there too. That's on the east side. On the west side is a place they call Snkeltína?, "up-on-top-side." That's where the campground is for the Kettle River people and the Okanogans. The place below the bridge is called Nlha?mína?, "close to the side." That's the Columbia River people's campground.

At the place Tkekxísxn', "crawl-over rock," north on the west side, the Kettle River people, the Okanogan people . . . all the tribes from Marcus on down, met. He took the salmon from there. He went up the Kettle River—went way up and then he made a falls.

4. Coyote Confesses

Coyote gathered all the people. Then he confessed to the chiefs. "When you guys wanted a smart man to go down and get the salmon, I was listening outside. I know you people don't like me because I'm tricky. But," he said, "I went down and got the salmon. Now," he said, "about the house—place to pray to the world. I made one," he told them, "down on the prairie. It'll be there when the people are descended here. That's where they'll go: the sick, the poor, for their health, for their future, for everything. Now," he said, "I'll show you people how I made it."

So, he made a sweathouse on both sides of the river. And he told them, "This is where you pray to the world, to the Creator." All right. The people said, "Thank you, Coyote. We don't dislike you, but you're awful, you're so tricky."

So Coyote said, "All right," he said. "This sweathouse is made. When the people come, that's where they will do their praying, do their wishing: for their health, for everything. Young and old."

He said, "Four directions—the food is there, every direction, the food. And the four colors of the earth." He said, "Now I'm finished." . . .

Coyote Brothers

This story here is about Coyote. He had a brother younger than him. Before they left home, their grandfather gave them two packages of power. They could do anything. They could wish for anything and it would come true. So, they travelled their own ways—travelled and used their power. Sometimes they tried something big and couldn't do it.

Finally, they met up at Hall Creek. They used to call that Ntsa?lí?m (Inchelium). Way up there another creek comes in from the north. They call that Ntektekiy'ám. Now, the English name for that creek is Buckhorn. There were a bunch of people there—a whole bunch of people camped there—hunting, gathering food for the winter. So, older Coyote peeked over and there were sure a lot of people there. He ducked back. Sitting there, he heard somebody coming down the hill. He looked up and, by God, there was his kid brother. Ahhh, they were happy.

They shook hands and said, "Where have you been?"

"Oh, I've been up Kettle River and up the Lake—Arrow Lakes—and all over. Where have you been?"

"Oh, I've been down on the flat, down here." Meaning around Davenport—Coulee City and all through there. "Along the Columbia. That's where I came back. And I came back up Ntsa?lkí?m (Inchelium). So here we met."

Older Coyote said, "Well, what kind of luck did you have all the way through? I could do a lot of things. But some big things, I can't do. I haven't got the power. I only have two bags." He had already figured out how he was going to swindle his kid brother—rip him off his power.

Younger Coyote said, "Well Coyote what can we do about it?"

The older said, "Don't call me Coyote. I'm not Coyote. You're the Coyote."

His kid brother told him, "No," he said, "we're both Coyotes. We have the same mother and same father, grandfathers, and grandmothers. We're all Coyotes."

The older said, "No. My name is different."

The younger asked, "What is your name?"

"Well, my name is Another One."

"No," he said, "You're a Coyote, just like me."

"No," he said, "you wanna prove it?"

"Sure," the kid brother said. "Sure. I want to prove it."

The older said, "All right, peek over the hill, towards the west."

They peeked over the hill. Gee, there were a lot of people there. They ducked back and the older Coyote said, "You run on that side hill. You see that little draw over there? You listen good to what they say, you listen good—they'll all holler `Coyote'. When you get on the side in that little draw, you wait there and listen good again. And if they call you Coyote and they call me Another One, then I'll win your two bags of power."

All right. They made a bet. They piled their bags of power there.

So Coyote, the young brother, ran on the side hill.

Everybody hollered, "Oh! Oh! Look, look at Coyote running there. That Coyote!"

He got out of sight in that little draw. He listened as his brother ran.

"Oh! Oh! Looka! Look! There's another one, 'nother one."

When the older brother got there, he said, "OK. You satisfied? My name is Another One. I'm not Coyote. You're the Coyote."

Kid brother said, "All right." So, he lost his two bags of power. And now, that's how we got these common coyotes out here. And they, the Indians, claim that the smart one is out on the sea somewhere. He'll be back here when the earth comes to an end. That's as far as that story goes.

Native Place Names on the Columbia Plateau

by Eugene S. Hunn

Native American peoples survived for millennia in the Pacific Northwest not solely because of their ingenious fishing and food processing technology, but by virtue of their detailed knowledge of the land and its resources. Education focused on *learning the land*, with dramatic accounts of the adventures of mythological creatures such as Coyote reinforcing their recall of critical information. For example, a single text dictated from memory by Jim Yoke, an Upper Cowlitz Indian, to Melville Jacobs in the late 1920s cites 275 named places and provides a capsule cultural annotation and resource inventory for each. The names were recalled systematically from a mental map of Yoke's home country.

Learning a landscape is not simply a matter of naming all the rivers and mountains. In fact, rivers and mountains per se are rarely named in Native American languages. The naming of such features of land reflects rather a peculiarly Western perspective—one set *above* or *outside*, rather than *within*, the landscape and motivated by the needs of a society bent upon dividing it up. From this perspective, features of the landscape are *objects* to be named. The Native American perspective, in contrast, emphasizes *places* where significant human-landscape interactions occur. Thus, while a few prominent peaks may have been named in the native languages— for example, taxúma (in the Puget Salish language) for Mount Rainier or lawiltayt-lá (in Sahaptin), literally "the smoker," for Mount St. Helens—other peaks of equal prominence were known simply as *patú*, a general Sahaptin term for "snow-capped summit."

The Native names now assigned to many Northwest rivers referred in the original languages to major villages or fishing sites on those rivers. Táytin (Tieton) named a spear-fishing site at the outlet of Clear Lake high up the Tieton River. In Sahaptin, látaxat (Klickitat) named the key Klickitat River fishery at the falls just above the river's mouth. Iyákima (Yakima), literally "the pregnant ones," indicated a string of hills near the present-day city of Yakima named for their resemblance to five pregnant women of a mythological account. Place names reveal a great deal about how a people appreciate the world they live in.

Josephine Andrews, a leading elder of the Yakima Indian Nation who was raised in the Naches River area, provided a key interpretation: naxcíis, literally "first water," refers to the fundamental role that the Naches basin's waters play as a source of life for the whole of the mid-Columbia plain. Her fears for the destruction of that water source brought into sharp focus the spiritual, as well as material, cost of a dam recently proposed on a tributary of the Naches.

The sacred mountain lalíik, the easternmost prominence of the Rattlesnake Hills which now mark the southern border of the Hanford Nuclear Reservation, marks an angle in the boundary of the lands ceded by the 1855 treaties. (In the Yakima treaty, the name of the mountain is misrepresented as "La Lac," and interpreted as a "lake.") Rising 3,000 feet above the river, the summit dominates the skyline for miles about. The Priest Rapids prophet smúxala (Smohalla) sought a visionary source of spirit power here. Today the mountain serves the elders as a weather vane; lingering snows on its summit augur a late spring growing season.

The ecological relationships forged by the Native cultures over the millennia of their occupation of this land are embodied in their place names. When and where may a plant or animal species be most reliably found or efficiently harvested? Success in hunting and gathering rests on a strategic choice of seasonal moves—a succession of camps established to provide a family access to a sufficient abundance and diversity of food and essential materials to sustain them each year. This is the *seasonal round* of those who live by gathering, fishing, and hunting; its precise shape is conditioned by the local landscape, but it is a cultural product nonetheless, a creation of the human mind.

Many places are named for particularly noteworthy plants, animals, or minerals found there or for related activities accomplished there. Some examples:

Kalamát, "yellow pond lily" (*Nuphar polysepalum*), names a meadow and pond in the southern Cascade Mountains of Washington where berries were picked in late summer; it is also the site of a historic Indian horse racing track. . . .

Tiskáya, "Skunk," as a character in myth, is the name of a mountain a few miles below present-day Packwood in Lewis County. . . .

More often, a plant or animal name is modified by a reduplication (doubling part or all of a word—this usually suggests small size or large numbers of something in Sahaptin) or by adding the possessive suffix -nmí or the suffix -as ("place of") or some variant thereof. Some examples:

Nánk-nank, "many cedars," for a place below Cowlitz Falls on the Cowlitz River.

Púusi or Púuspuusi, "of junipers" or "many junipers," for present Redmond, Oregon, and for a dip-netting site just below Alderdale, Klickitat County, Washington. . . .

Taxús-as, "Indian hemp place," for lower Crab Creek, Grant County; it is reputed that

Indian hemp (*Apocynum cannabinum*) here was of such fine quality that battles were fought to control it. . . .

Sapawilalat-pamá, "for set-netting," another site at Celilo Falls, where large-mouthed dip-nets were fixed by lines beneath a fish jumping place.

Place name nomenclature always reflects an individual point of view. An exhaustive inventory of a region's place names, however, will considerably exceed any single individual's repertory.

Celilo Falls

A few miles below the mouth of the Deschutes a basalt ridge cuts across the Columbia River's course. This is Celilo Falls. [The Celilo Falls area is now flooded by the Dalles Dam.] Here and for the next ten miles the full force of the Columbia is shunted through a series of narrow passages. . . . At high water in June the river surges up and over these obstructions; but when the flood recedes, channels open through which the salmon force their way, driven to return to spawn in their natal streams. The salmon surge past in sharp pulses: spring Chinook salmon in early May, blueback salmon in July, then summer runs of Chinook and steelhead followed in early September by the heavy fall Chinook run and in October by silver salmon. The complex configuration of channels and eddies on this stretch of the Columbia provided excellent fishing for men armed with dip-nets, gaffhooks, or spears. A large surplus of fish was dried and stored for later use or for barter and trade. Local fishermen hosted several thousand visitors during summer and fall while they waited for the runs to pass. The region of the great falls and the dalles saw a great emporium that brought together peoples within a radius of several hundred miles.

James Selam, a fluent native speaker of the Columbia River Sahaptin language, was born in 1918 and raised between Rock Creek and the John Day River some thirty miles upriver from Celilo Falls. His father shared rights by inheritance to use certain fishing stations at the Great Falls. Thus, James Selam witnessed Native fishing practices there as a child and young adult during the 1920s and 1930s. By consulting a map that showed the contours of the falls before they were inundated by the Dalles Dam, James Selam recalled 15 named sites within the single square mile encompassing the falls. By his own admission his recollection of named sites there is far from complete, yet the details he can still recall graphically illustrate the complexity of traditional geographic perceptions at this key fishery. Most of these names denote fishing sites that belonged to particular families and were often named for the fishing practices appropriate to each site.

The Columbia River itself is known throughout the Sahaptin speech area simply as nc'i-wána, "big river." Some major villages are occupied during the summer, others during the winter or year-around. These village names apply not only to the villages themselves, but also to the region immediately surrounding the village. As such, the term might subsume other named sites.

The name of a village might also be used for the group of people who lived there. Thus, wayám was the summer village on the Oregon side of the river at Celilo Falls; the people of that village were the wayam-láma, though they retired during the winter months to the more sheltered village site of tq'ux at the mouth of the Deschutes River or to a village just up the Deschutes called wanwáwi.

Their closest neighbors were the sk'in-láma, residents of the permanent village of sk'in on the Washington shore at the falls. This village, built on a sandy beach just below the falls, is named for a prominent rock formation on the Washington shore at the lip of the falls. This rock resembled a cradleboard—which is the literal meaning of sk'in—and alludes to a myth of the origin of salmon.

In this myth, the Swallow Sisters (five mythological beings in the form of birds) have dammed the river, preventing the salmon from migrating upstream to spawn and thus depriving the upriver peoples of their livelihood. The mythological superhero Coyote, disguised as a baby, straps himself to a cradleboard and floats down the river to Celilo. There he deceives the Swallow Sisters who take him in as a foundling. While the sisters are away digging roots in the nearby hills (as the women of sk'in families still do), Coyote destroys the dam and releases the salmon to return to the streams of their birth. The cradle-shaped rock for which this village and its people were named was destroyed during construction of the railroad bridge across the west end of the falls.

Lewis and Clark described Celilo Falls: "The waters is divided into Several narrow chanels which pass through a hard black rock forming Islands of rocks at this Stage of the water, on those Islands of rocks . . . I observe great numbers of Stacks of pounded Salmon neetly preserved. . . ." The two largest of those islands are known locally as "Kiska" and "Big Island." "Papoose," "Chief," and "Standing" are local names for smaller islands that split the main channel between Big Island and the mainland at the head of the falls on the Oregon side.

Native nomenclature—as James Selam recalls it—departs again from Euro-American conventions in that the islands themselves were not named. "Kiska Island" is a corruption of the Sahaptin term kis, literally "stinking," which denoted a fishing site on the northwest side of the island at which dead fish became trapped in a pool on the rocks, where they decomposed. Kis was opposite a prominent rocky point on the Washington shore known as núsnu, "nose." The rock called sk'in, "cradleboard," was just upstream, as were two fishing sites named for the fishing methods used there. At tayxayt-pamá, "for spear fishing," flat pale-colored rocks just beneath the surface of the current highlighted the migrating fish so they could be easily speared. At sapawilatat-pamá, "for set-netting," fish leaped from the water in their efforts to surmount the falls. A wide-mouthed net tied with lines caught the fish as they fell back.

Big Island was called simply amáwi, "island." It was located immediately opposite the village of wayám (about where the Celilo Longhouse stands today) and was reached by canoe from the wayám landings. About the turn of the century, an overhead cable was stretched to Big Island from the Seufert brothers' Tumwater fish wheel and fish processing operation on the Oregon shore to transport Native fishermen and their catches. Drying sheds were built on Big Island to serve a number of fishing stations on the island's northeast point, but James Selam could not recall the names of these sites. "Chief Island" was so called because Chief Tommy Thompson, last of the traditional salmon chiefs—leaders with the spiritual authority to regulate fishing—had had his fishing places, collectively designated *swáycas*, there.

"Standing Island" was named for a fishing site at the channel between it and Chief Island. It was known in Sahaptin as awxanáycas, which means something like "standing at the lip of the falls." Here seven men standing could dip-net salmon together. The fishermen swept their long-handled dip nets with the current, feeling for fish in the roiling water. Whenever a fish was netted, the successful fisherman stepped back to be replaced by another.

A small rock between the northeast corner of Standing Island and the Oregon shore was called lmáma, "old woman." Just above was an island at the top of the falls where I. H. Taffe set up three fish wheels and a cannery about 1890. Just below these wheels was pác'pas, "channel" a good site for catching "ells" (Pacific lamprey). "Gaff-hooking

place," q'íyak-awas, was located on the north shore of Standing Island. . . .

Indian Heaven
James Selam's family, by virtue of their kinship ties to sk'in, fished the summer and fall salmon runs at Celilo. From there they trekked each summer to their huckleberry camp southeast of Mount St. Helens to a place called áyun-ás, "lovage place" (for ayun, *Ligusticum canbyi*, a medicinal root), in the area now known as Indian Heaven. Here they could escape the oppressive August heat of the Columbia Valley. The women gathered and dried a winter's supply of huckleberries and wild blueberries while the men hunted deer or ranged down into the Columbia Gorge to fish at the mouths of the White Salmon, Little White Salmon, and Wind rivers. According to James Selam, each community had a traditionally recognized camping and berry-picking area on this high, forested plateau. The Klickitats camped ten miles north of áyun-as at pswawas-wáakul, "saw-like," now called the Sawtooth Huckleberry Fields. All gathered to socialize, trade, and race horses at kalamát, "yellow pond-lily," a broad meadow astride the Klickitat Trail.

Pond lilies are rare in high mountain meadows; however, when James Selam and I hiked in—bushwhacking along the overgrown path he had taken with his parents over 50 years before—there were a few pond lilies in a shallow tarn at the meadow's edge. An incongruous heron flushed squawking at our approach. Although the pond lily was a staple food of the Klamath people of southern Oregon, it was not used by local Native groups. Thus, this meadow's namesake was memorable not so much for its economic value but for its surprising presence far from its expected haunts.

. . . For native peoples, topographic forms may reflect deeper mythical realities. At a spot just off State Highway 14, high above the Columbia River opposite the mouth of the Deschutes, James Selam indicated the exact spot where Coyote hid when he taunted nayslá, the "Swallowing Monster" that dwelled long ago in a deep pool in the river below. Selam pointed to a narrow defile below us that led down to the water. This had been gouged by Coyote as he was dragged into the monster's cavernous maw. Coyote found all sorts of people trapped inside. Grizzly Bear, Wolf, Rattlesnake, all sorts of powerful beings were powerless to escape. But Coyote had come prepared. He pulled out tinder, kindling, and flint, built a fire beneath the monster's heart, and proceeded to hack at its moorings with his knife. Coyote led the Animal People to freedom from the belly of the dying beast, some escaping by its mouth, others in the opposite direction.

Note: Indian words are written in a phonemic alphabet based on Bruce Rigsby's Ph.D. dissertation, *Linguistic Relations in the Southern Plateau* (University of Oregon, Eugene, 1965), p. 156. Consonants with a superscripted apostrophe are "glottalized," pronounced with an explosive burst of air from the throat. . . . The q is a "k" sound pronounced far back toward the throat. The x is likewise pronounced far back toward the throat, but sounds more like the "ch" of Scottish "loch.". . . A question mark without the dot is a "glottal stop." The accent mark indicated the most heavily stressed syllable of a polysyllabic word.

Riverworlds

The Sweep of Cultures and the Columbia

by James P. Ronda

He never saw the Columbia, never even got close. But Henry David Thoreau, that leafy wizard of eastern woods and rivers, read everything he could lay his hands on about the great River of the West. He listened to the Columbia's voices and once exclaimed, "What a piece of wonder a river is." We have had our river philosophers: Mark Twain, Woody Guthrie, John Wesley Powell, and James Dickey. With them we have gone up the Hudson, down the Mississippi, and across the wide Missouri. With them we have marched the Platte, run the thundering Colorado, and eyed the flecks of yellow glinting in the south fork of the American. But it was Thoreau, that great explorer who hardly ever left home, who can teach us a river philosophy. This is what he said about the worlds of rivers: rivers are "emblems" of our deepest longings; rivers are the waters of prophecy, telling us who we are and what we might become; rivers carry us into the interiors of continents; exploring rivers we explore ourselves; rivers are "the constant lure . . . to distant enterprises and adventure."

Prompted by the river philosophers, we need to think again about rivers and cultures in America. Too often we see the river as something running through places, not as a place itself. We need to let the river occupy more space in our imagination. We need to let the Columbia River, any river, be what it is a place fixed in time and space. There is a tension, a peculiar contradiction in this. We tend to envision place as a fixed point. Rivers seem to us like threads, running through the fabric of places. We imagine rivers as highways to or through the places of our dreams.

Perhaps now we need to integrate land and water by thinking about riverworlds. This is what the trendy might call an ecosystem or a piece of the biosphere. Let's be simpler and say that the air, earth, fire, water, and all the creatures therein make a riverworld.

So far, this discussion has been properly metaphysical and appropriately vague. But how do we come to understand riverworlds? Where do we stand to witness the powerful complexity of the Columbia River worlds? A little more than a century ago our greatest river thinker, Mark Twain, asked the same question: How could he come to terms with his past on the Mississippi and bring it alive for a present audience. Twain's answer came in his *Life on the Mississippi,* a book filled with haunting beauty and restless energy. His advice: plant yourself somewhere and from that vantage point watch the river's procession of people and events, dreams and schemes. For Twain, there were three lookout points–the town of Hannibal on the Mississippi, the pilot house on the Texas-deck of a river steamboat, and on the raft with Huck and Jim. Twain puts us there and we see the world of the river in all its changing moods, all its fearsome moral complexity.

Where shall we plant ourselves to see the sweep of cultures, the currents of change on the Columbia? We might settle in the Clatsop village of Neahkeluk on Point Adams. We might join Lewis and Clark off the beaten track at Fort Clatsop. Or we could put in at Astoria and watch the change from fur to fish, and on to tourism. But considering the whole range of human experience in this riverworld, there seems only one logical place–The Dalles, that extraordinary fracture point in riverworld geography and cultures. Imagine a series of snapshots taken there beginning in 1800 and running to the beginning of our century. Each photo might reveal awesome, sometimes disturbing changes wrought by waves of white outsiders, new goods, and powerful technologies. These photos might reveal the eternal continuity of the river. Taken together, they would comprise a portrait of the Columbia River world.

In 1800 The Dalles was a place of extraordinary activity and human enterprise. Here, where the river roared through the Long and Short Narrows, was the center of a vast trade network. What anthropologists have since come to call the Pacific-Plateau system involved exchanging huge quantities of dried salmon for other food and trade goods. Stretching from the Pacific Coast to Nez Perce homelands and linked to the Missouri River Indian villages by way of the Shoshoni Rendezvous, the network joined Chinookan and Sahaptian-speaking peoples in an intricate set of personal and economic relationships. Through the trade system flowed not only fish, wappato bread, buffalo robes, and European goods, but also games, songs, and stories.

Geography, in the form of a dramatic narrowing of the Columbia at The Dalles and the resulting creation of ideal fishing stations, conspired with climate–warm, dry winds blowing up the gorge–to make the Indian villages around the Long and Short Narrows, in William Clark's words, "great marts of trade." The Wishram Indians lived on the north bank of The Dalles; the Wascos occupied sites on the north side of the river. Although trading and fishing took place from Celilo Falls down to The Dalles, the most intense bargaining was done at the main Wishram village. When Lewis and Clark visited the village in late October 1805, they found some 20 large wooden plank houses, each holding three Wishram extended families.

What no visitor could miss were the towering stacks of dried salmon. Clark estimated that there were 10,000 pounds, pointing up the vast quantities of goods exchanged throughout the system. Trading took place from spring through fall during the major salmon runs, with most activity reserved for the fall season. During September and October, dried fish and roots were freshly prepared and in abundant supply. To The Dalles trade fair came nearby Yakimas and Teninos as well as more distant Umatillas, Walulas, and Nez Perces. Local Sahaptians brought to The Dalles food products, including meat, roots, and berries. At the trading places, Wishram brokers exchanged those items for dried salmon and European cloth and ironware. Distant Sahaptians–especially the Nez Perces, who had access to the plains–brought skin clothing, horses, and buffalo meat. Less interested in fish than their Columbia cousins, the plateau people were drawn to The Dalles in search of European goods, especially metal and beads.

Centered at The Dalles and with one arm stretching east, The Dalles system also reached west down the Columbia to the coastal Chinookans. The Pacific people brought to The Dalles a variety of European goods obtained from maritime fur traders, as well as indigenous crops. Guns, blankets, clothing, and the prized blue beads–all came up The Dalles. Heading upriver in their graceful canoes, the lower Chinookans also transported wappato roots to be pounded and made into a tasty bread. Once at The Dalles, Chinookans traded for dried salmon, buffalo meat, and valuable bear grass used in making cooking baskets and the distinctive Northwest Coast hats.

The full flavor of a rendezvous at The Dalles must have been an unforgettable experience. The smell of drying fish hung in the fall air, and clouds of fleas and gnats hovered everywhere. At peak trading times, some 3,000 Indians gathered for the rituals of bargain and exchange. But those festive fall days promised more than a redistribution of wealth. Here native people met old friends, made new ones, and heard the latest news. Gambling, socializing, and sporting for the opposite sex were all essential features of the trading days. Fur trader Alexander Ross, who saw The Dalles system before it was swept away by disease and white invasion, caught the spirit of those high times. "The Long Narrows," wrote Ross, "is the great emporium or mart of the Columbia and the general theatre of gambling and roguery."

Standing at The Dalles, any visitor–Indian or non-Indian–could see the visible signs of so vast a trading system. What was not so readily apparent in this riverworld was power and politics. On the Missouri, Teton Sioux bands gained and exercised power by controlling goods moving up and down the river. Upper Chinookans such as the Skilloots did not have the military power possessed by the Tetons, but they were willing to resort to force to protect their accustomed place as middlemen in the trading system. Just how far Indians from The Dalles to the Cascades would go to defend their place in the network would be revealed in 1812 and 1814, when river Indians fought pitched battles with fur traders for passage on the Columbia. Such was the contest of cultures as bearded strangers began to push and paddle into the Columbia River world.

With the arrival of Euro-Americans, the very meaning of The Dalles and the riverworld began to change. Native people saw that narrowing of the river as a convenient meeting place, a grand market center. To them, The Dalles meant opportunity. Euro-Americans, whether merchants, traders, miners, or settlers, looked at The Dalles and saw a barrier, a challenge, something to overcome, to portage around. In the late 1820s, as the Hudson's Bay Company expanded its operations under the leadership of Sir George Simpson and Dr. John McLoughlin, the "Honourable Company" ran afoul of native toll keepers at The Dalles. During the winter of 1829-1830, The Dalles saw its first non-Indian trading post, a temporary Hudson's Bay Company affair put up to meet a brief American challenge.

But these merchant comings and goings did not immediately alter the fundamental character of The Dalles and the riverworld. It was still a world of business, whoever the brokers and whatever the mode of exchange. The past is never absent from the present. The traders' world began to shift in the mid-1830s with the Protestant missionary invasion of the riverworld. The evangelical rush to save Indian souls and the Reverend Samuel Parker's reconnaissance of mission fields ripe for harvest are familiar stories. In March 1838, The Dalles witnessed a new kind of visitor, one who traded in spiritual coin.

The Wascopam Methodist mission brought permanent white settlers, plough agriculture, new building styles, and an ideology that mixed evangelical Christianity and expansionist American nationalism. What the mission families brought were social and economic tools and techniques that would set in motion a transformation of The Dalles and the riverworld. Within a year there were five acres of wheat, potatoes, and assorted vegetables.

When Joseph Drayton and a party from the United States Exploring Expedition visited The Dalles in early July 1841, there were signs of both old ways and new. The Methodist Mission, now three families strong, boasted two log-and-board houses, a small barn, and a scattering of outbuildings. The settlement's irrigated fields offered crops of wheat and potatoes. But The Dalles still represented a native world, the world of fish and trade. Recalling London's great fish market, Drayton called The Dalles "the Billingsgate of Oregon." Indian horses and fish drying racks were everywhere. They were constant reminders of a world on the brink of profound change–change toward the riverworld of the mission settlers with their books, board houses, and potatoes.

It is easy to think of the 1840s as the Age of the Oregon Question and migration to the Willamette Valley. But we can get lost too quickly in the tangles of great power diplomacy and quick generalizations about the Oregon Trail. Seeing it from The Dalles' perspective, how was the riverworld changing? When John Charles Fremont's expedition came to The Dalles in November 1843, there was the obligatory mention of the Narrows. But for Fremont–ever the agent of empire– what counted was the mission settlement. Substantial buildings, a school, and cleared fields filled his vision of the Columbia. Looking at the landscape–and Fremont really meant the *land*scape–he had this to say: "The valley [carries] the cheerful and busy air of civilization, and had in our eyes an appearance of abundant and enviable comfort."

It was this landed vision–one that Fremont did so much to promote–that set loose a great rush of humanity bound for the Oregon Country. That migration, with all its rippling consequences, enveloped The Dalles. Emigrant families tied up at the place and, after the construction of the Barlow Road, pressed on by wagon to the Willamette country. If St. Louis was the gateway to the West, then The Dalles quickly became the gateway to the Northwest. Jumping-off place, provisioning point, rest stop–The Dalles became all those things. Nathan Olney's log store was just one sign of things to come. The emigrant invasion meant conflict with native people, conflict that brought two companies of the Regiment of Mounted Riflemen. Garrisoned at Camp Drum, later called Fort Dalles, the troops were a visible sign of American dominion. The post's barracks, storehouses, stable, and sawmill gave tangible expression to a growing American pres-

ence. As at The Dalles, so elsewhere–the riverworld was becoming part of the American empire.

That empire meant politics–the creation of Wasco County and the platting of The Dalles city. It meant the coming of a capitalist, profit-driven economy based on intensive agriculture, stock raising, provisioning the emigrant trade, and portaging around the Narrows and Celilo Falls. The portage road was soon choked with traffic as oxen, mules, and horses strained against their loads. When census takers came to count heads in 1860, the tally sheets showed 1,340 residents at The Dalles. And the whole riverworld was about to be jolted by a gold rush.

The business of The Dalles had always been business, whether the merchants traded fish or buffalo or sold goods to emigrants. There was a kind of underlying continuity that linked native past to the American present. But the Clearwater River Gold Rush of the early 1860s shattered that continuity once and for all. Gold strikes in the upper Clearwater country meant boom times at both The Dalles and Walla Walla. One historian of the California Gold Rush called his book *The World Rushed In*. And that is just what happened at The Dalles. Law and justice broke down at The Dalles city in early 1862 as a stampede of miners and hangers-on surged into the riverworld. And for a moment there was mob rule. Once order was restored, The Dalles became a major provisioning and trans-shipping point. Dreaming of a monopoly on the Columbia, the Oregon Steam Navigation Company now made bumper profits, as freight and passenger rates soared.

In the spring of 1863, work was finished on a portage railroad. Its locomotive, properly named after riverboat captain and master entrepreneur John C. Ainsworth, now whistled in the age of the iron horse. A decade and a half later, the 14-mile Dalles and Celilo Railroad boasted 3 engines, 46 freight cars, and 2 passenger cars–all valued at $700,000. Gold rush prosperity sparked a Dalles building boom, as solid stone and brick shops, homes, schools, and churches filled the familiar grid that marks so many American settlements. In the full bloom of enthusiasm, work began on a branch of the United States mint, and local entrepreneurs talked confidently about starting a woolen mill.

For better or worse, the Columbia River world was not part of the larger American world–a place where boom and bust ruled the day. And gold proved a flash in the pan. The census of 1870 told the dismal story of a boom gone bust and booster promises turned sour. The Dalles city population had shrunk to 942, the buildings at Fort Dalles were empty, the mint building stood half-built, and the proud industrial experiment, the Wasco Woolen Manufacturing Company, slid into bankruptcy. Only the busy shops of the Oregon Steam Navigation Company promised some economic relief.

In fact, what brought The Dalles a measure of security and prosperity was the revival of the landed vision that had so captivated Fremont and the Oregon emigrants of the 1840s. At the end of the 1870s, as Indian resistance finally collapsed, a land rush south of The Dalles and across the river in the Swale renewed the area's vitality. What gold could not provide, grain would. By the turn of the century, The Dalles had become the very image of a late Victorian American city. Symbols of arrival were everywhere: an electric light system, well-stocked shops, and an impressive opera house. The 1910 census put it all with numerical precision: 4,880 residents busy at everything from machinist to druggist to housewife and schoolteacher.

In 1805, The Dalles symbolized a riverworld linked by trade and great merchant fairs. Now, a century later, the trade was in grain and the network was steel rails, telegraph wires, and steamboat routes. This is not the story of progress, but of cultural variation and technological innovation–all within the limits set by the river. As the river defined the original native people, so it would come to define the new natives, whether those new natives were soldiers or farmers, railroaders or windsurfers.

So we have come full circle. Riverworlds are as changing as the river itself. How shall we begin to understand those profound changes? We need the historian's backward glance, the geographer's sense of space, the archaeologist's grasp of objects, and the folklorist's sensitivity to the spoken and re-membered word. What remarkable and telling things we might set side by side: wappato bread and biscuit tins; dried fish and sides of beef; elk skin shirts and woolen long johns; plank houses and opera houses. Or perhaps we might summon for a curtain call the cast of characters in this drama of riverworlds. Traders—both Indian and white—and sol-diers, missionaries, emigrants, boatmen, housewives, and teamsters. The cast was and remains as varied as the American expe-rience itself.

Imagine the sounds of the riverworlds; conjure up a soundscape. We need to hear again, if only through the ear of the imagina-tion, the roar of the river through the Nar-rows, the voices of fishing folk and traders, and the shouts, songs, stories, and laughter of trading days. What now blows only in the wind of memory are the whistles of steam-boats and locomotives, the singing whine of the flanged wheel on the steel rail. Hear again the creak and groan of overlander wagons and the crack of a driver's whip as a wagon and 12-horse hitch roll into town. Would that we could screen out the sounds of Union Pacific freights and diesel 18-wheel-ers on Interstate 84. Then we might catch the sounds of more distant times.

Some 60 years ago, Woody Guthrie, the poet laureate of the Columbia, wrote the anthem of the river. "Roll on, Columbia" is one of a handful of American songs that transcend time and place to reach us all. With Guthrie, we might ask: What rolls on the Columbia, and what roles does the river play in our shared past and common future? The riverworld, a living place, is a spark to the imagination. "To live by a great river," writes John Haines, "is to be kept in the heart of things."

We always come back to the river, that energizing, life-giving force. We are drawn to it, and somehow feel uncomfortable when away. We may dream dreams in dry places, but it is the riverworld that has come to be the emblem of our deepest, most enduring experiences. A river journey may be into the heart of darkness, or it may be our deliverance. What a wonder a river is. Roll on, Columbia.

Encounter on the Columbia
An Inner History of Trade and Its Consequences
by William L. Lang

Revolutionary events in the course of human history do not occur often, but when they do the earth seems to turn at a different rate, the world looks new, and the pace of change quickens. Five centuries ago, one of those revolutionary events, one long in developing but dramatic in its unfolding, altered world history through geographical discovery. The dynamic consequences of the European exploration and colonization of North and South America changed the New World as fundamentally as it did the Old. In the new lands, the change was measured in technologies and goods introduced, in diseases imported, in cultures disrupted, and in people enslaved. In Europe, it was measured in capitalism stimulated, in specie imported, and in politics revolutionized. By whatever measurement, the Columbian discoveries and their consequences qualify as revolutionary and world-changing.

The Encounter between the "discovered" and the "discoverers" created a whirlwind legacy, a legacy that brought a few nations wealth and power and extended well beyond those nations' aspirations. Some three centuries after Columbus, another battalion of discoverers, emboldened by a new science and sailing for commerce, brought the legacy of the Encounter into the waters of the North Pacific. Ship captains pursuing wealth in otter pelts and knowledge about this remote region were the first to inform the outside world about its resources and people. Included on their charts was a great river that flowed from the continental interior and emptied into the Pacific at about the 46th parallel. It was the "Great River of the West,"

first identified by Bruno de Hezeta in 1775 and named the Columbia in 1792 by American sea captain Robert Gray. Gray tentatively explored the river's mouth and later that year British Lieutenant William Broughton charted about 100 miles of the Columbia's course. These explorations triggered a half-century of encounters between Indian and non-Indian peoples on the Columbia that revolutionized the region.

The Columbia is a long and powerful river course. Heading in lakes at the base of the Canadian Rockies and flowing more than 1,200 miles to the ocean, the Columbia cuts through a dozen or more separate natural environments that afforded sustenance and brought wealth to thousands of Native Americans who lived within the circle of its influence. That world, created by the nexus of river, land, and people—a world preexisting the contact between whites and Indians—was rich and complex. Its richness can be counted in the number of tribes and in the variety of peoples who drew strength from the Columbia. From the Sanpoil and Kootenai on its upper courses to the Chinook and Cowlitz of the lower river, the lifeways, language, and material culture of Indian groups were as differentiated as the landscape. On the lower river, from the Cascades to the sea, Indian groups relied on one of the world's great fisheries and prospered better than perhaps any other native group on the continent. On the Columbia Plateau, through which the river runs in a great basaltic gorge, more sparsely settled Native American tribes sustained themselves by utilizing what the environment offered.

19

Grasping the importance and dimensions of the Encounter on the Columbia begins with gaining some understanding of the Native American world that the white intruders discovered there. It was a complex and sophisticated world infused with natural and supernatural forces. Indian people lived in an environment that offered riches but also strained human ingenuity and tested their intelligence and resourcefulness. They struck an accommodation with this nurturing and demanding environment, an agreement that emphasized respect and underscored knowledge. As anthropologist Eugene Hunn has shown, Indians knew their land in a most intimate detail. The taxonomy of plant resources–as reflected in the names Indians gave each species, sub-species, and seasonal variations–describes a complex world with great sophistication. Plant names carried with them descriptions, locations, harvest or germination seasons, and their uses as food or medicines. The names recorded the smallest fragments of utilitarian import, the incidental but crucial characteristics of thousands of plants and other food resources.

Indian society was similarly complex and sophisticated. Relationships in families and village groups on the Columbia rested on a complicated kinship system that emphasized the equitable and respectful treatment of individuals. Those relationships informed Indians' lives nearly as much as their interaction with the natural world did. And behind it all, Native Americans believed in a spiritual world that coexisted and intermingled with the natural world. Human beings and the society they created existed on a cooperative basis with the rest of creation, and that translated into complex rules of behavior between people and people, people and the land, and people and the spiritual world.

For Native Americans on the Columbia, the Encounter with whites began long before they actually saw or met them. The precursor was often virulent disease that spread upstream from the coast, shocking and baffling Native Americans as unremediated illness took life after life. As early as 1775, smallpox claimed more than 15 percent of some tribes along the river. Subsequent ravages of smallpox, measles, and malaria decimated most tribes by the 1830s, leaving only a fraction of the population that had existed before contact with whites. By the time Meriwether Lewis and William Clark explored the region in 1805-1806, probably half of the native population had succumbed to disease. It was, as one scholar has described it, an unprecedented holocaust.

Trade was a more benign interaction. It had been the first point and purpose of contact between the sea captains and coastal tribes, and it quickly dominated their intercourse. Through the extensive intertribal trade network, European-made glass, metal, and cloth items were exchanged from tribe to tribe. The central place in this network on the Columbia was The Dalles—"the great emporium," as fur trader Alexander Ross called it—where Indians throughout the Northwest had traded for hundreds of years. Trade at The Dalles was so rich that in 1805, as they came down the Columbia, Lewis and Clark met Indians who thought whites must be living at The Dalles because of the prevalence of trade goods there. The explorers also saw evidence of the trade's penetration into the interior. Near the Walla Walla River, the explorers met Indians who had "large blue and white beeds [and] bracelets of Brass, Copper," and later downstream near the mouth of the Deschutes River they encountered Indians with "two Scarlet and a blue cloth blanket, also a Salors Jacket."

Trade had wicked up the Columbia so rapidly that Lewis and Clark, who were among the first whites to encounter Indians along the river, met the advance legions of their own civilization deep in the wilderness. They took careful notes, recording their observations of existing trade among Indian tribes and the possibility of trade with the United States. They did this in obedience to President Thomas Jefferson's instructions to study Indian peoples and record "the names of the nations and their numbers" and especially "the articles of commerce they may need or furnish and to what extent." As James Ronda has brilliantly explained, trade and the potential for trade agreements with Indians became a central element, if not the crucial factor, in Lewis and Clark's relationships with Native Americans. For Lewis and Clark, friendly relations with Indians presaged longer term commercial agreements, making trade itself the principal medium of intercourse between the cultures.

Trade, perhaps more than any other activity between whites and Indians, became the arena of common focus and exchange of information. Native Americans and traders observed each other keenly, drew conclusions from their impressions, and ultimately characterized each other in the process. For decades before Lewis and Clark ventured west, North Pacific Coast Indians had called Americans in ships "Boston Men," reflecting as much the whites' focus on trade as their geographical origins. For many Columbia River Indians, whites and trade were nearly synonymous.

In trade, whether between the sea captains at the river's mouth or upriver with Lewis and Clark and the later fur men, both Indians and whites focused on the exchange. In these instances, the Encounter put individuals of different cultures—one far from his home territory and the other squarely in his native place—face to face, with objects of exchange between them. Individually they assigned value and bargained, taking what they desired and what they could get. White traders commonly expressed gleeful surprise at the high value Indians placed on items that seemed mere trinkets. Indians traded what whites wanted in return for as much in trade

goods as bargaining allowed.

Whites often commented on how keenly Indians traded and the hard bargains they drove. But the Indians' trade practices also confused them. Lewis and Clark recorded that a lively trade between Indians and coastal traders had developed in guns, kettles, wire, fishinghooks, buttons, and other items in exchange for animal skins and food, suggesting some equanimity and perhaps even advantage for the Indians. But juxtaposed to this observation Lewis also wrote: "The natives are extravegantly fond of the most common cheap blue and white beads, of moderate size, or such that from 50 to 70 will weigh one penneyweight. . . . for these beads they will dispose any article they possess." His critique scolds them as foolish even as the explorers considered Indians to be crafty and intelligent traders, full of guile.

David Thompson, the great land geographer and North West Company trader who first met and traded with Indians near the source of the Columbia at Columbia Lake, also critiqued Indian trading. Writing about his experiences among Walla Walla Indians in 1811, he observed that the chief hoped Thompson would "bring [them] arms, arrow shods of iron, axes, knives and many other things which you [Thompson] have and which we very much want." It was the women, Thompson observed, who wanted "blue beads, rings and other trifles." Exchanging these items was an assumed part of the costs of trade, to Thompson a necessary but distracting aspect of the process.

If the trade required these involved exchanges, Thompson and other fur traders like Alexander Ross and Gabriel Franchere of the Pacific Fur Company grumbled but accepted it. They focused instead on their objective, acquiring fur pelts—preferably otter, beaver, and fox—which their employers desired. For the Indians, trade meant opportunity to exchange anything they had for articles they desired, and that meant guns, metal, brightly hued cloth, beads, and more. The trade, seen from the Indians' viewpoint, looked like the open end of the Horn of Cornucopia. The whites saw it as the narrow end.

But in the case of Lewis and Clark, as Ronda tells us, the explorers were not so focused on trading with Indians as they were in establishing agreements to trade. They sought some basis upon which to build a trade. Among the Mandan and Hidatsa, far to the east of the Columbia, that meant halting war and establishing peace as a basis for trade. On the Columbia, it meant discovering the right articles to trade and finding Indians who were trustworthy in trade. For David Thompson, when he established the first trading establishment on the Columbia River near its source in 1807, the problem was not cessation of war but the arming of friends.

Thompson's incursion west the Rockies and his traffic in weapons with his trading partners threatened the balance of power among Indian tribes in the region. Through it all, he kept his purpose clear and used any method he could to strike the bargain. Four years later and down the Columbia, Thompson told assembled Indians who were eager for trade: "We had armed all the natives, particularly the Salish and Kootenays, and that as soon as possible we should do the same to all his people, that the way we brought the goods at present obliged us to cross high mountains and through hostile people, that we now sought a short safe way, by which all the articles they wanted would come in safety."

What Thompson and other fur traders wanted was not unlike what all European traders desired. They wanted stable trading conditions and as many advantages as possible in support of their trade. Trading in another's country, the fur men tried always to control access to their trading partners, as Thompson suggested, and to find the best means to conduct trade. In that pursuit, Lewis and Clark, Thompson, Ross, and the other men who had first contact with the Indians on the Columbia preferred establishing relations with one man from each tribe, someone they could identify as chief. This desire, whether it be part of negotiations for trade or a matter of war and peace, became a bugbear for whites who wanted stable relations with Indians. The singularity of leadership and especially the authority to speak for all Indians who wished to trade at any opportunity did not exist in Native American cultures. Almost invariably, white traders frustrated themselves in their insistence on chieftain brokers for their ambitious trade, while they continued to grumble and resist the free-wheeling trading practices most Indians used.

The white traders drew their own conclusions, as did the Indians. The opinions that fur men held about their partners in these exchanges on the Columbia, however, disclose a more serious difficulty in the trade and take us deeper into an ambivalence inherent in the Encounter. The acerbic Ross Cox, a Pacific Fur Company trader, wrote that, in his opinion, "the good qualities of these Indians are few; their vices many. Industry, patience, sobriety, and ingenuity nearly comprise the former; while in the latter may be classed, thieving, lying, incontinence, gambling, and cruelty. They are also perfect hypocrites." Lewis and Clark hurled some of the same epithets at Columbia River Indians, especially those along the lower river.

At The Dalles in 1811, Thompson puzzled at the actions of a party of Indians who attempted to block their passage and gouge from them some kind of payment. He told them they were being foolish to threaten his group. "We expressed our surprise that we who had come so far should meet such hard treatment; that we came to supply their wants, and not to kill, or be killed, and if they continued to threaten our lives, they must not expect to see us again." The game these Indians played baffled Thompson: "We hardly knew what to make of these people; they appeared a mixture of kindness and treachery; willingly rendering every service required, and performing well what they undertook, but demanding exorbitant prices for their services, and dagger in hand ready to enforce their demands . . . they steal all they can lay their hands on, and nothing can be gotten from them which they have stolen."

It was the stealing that especially bothered the traders. At Celilo Falls on the Columbia, Lewis and Clark complained that they had to situate their camp "for the protection of our stores from thieft, which we were more fearfull of, than their arrows." And far up the Columbia at Fort Okanogan, Alexander Ross labeled Indians "a people who delight in perfidy! Perfidy is the system of savages, treachery and cunning the instruments of their power, and cruelty and bloodshed the policy of their country." The basis of trade, these men expected and believed, had to be some measure of honesty. The Indians' theft of trade goods and stores seemed foolishly destructive. Ross and others like him seem to be asking: What is wrong? Why do they act this way? Do they know that this damages, even negates, trade?

For the Indian traders, the view was much different. Trade was important to them, but it was less important, much less, than other aspects of their lives. In their exchanges with whites, threats, posturing, offers of food, ritual blessings, and even theft often intermingled. American and English traders received conflicting messages and drew confused conclusions. Indians seemed to welcome the whites and what they could provide Indians, but they also rejected them by stealing what the whites brought and suddenly altering the rules of the trade. During the cold and damp winter of 1805-1806 at Fort Clatsop, Lewis reflected on his expedi-

tion's experiences with the Indians, writing in his journal about the need to caution his men against a too easy association with Indians: ". . . for notwithstanding their [the Indians'] friendly disposition, their great averice and hope of plunder might induce them to be treacherous . . . we well know, that the treachery of the aborigenes of America and the too great confidence of our country men in their sincerity and friendship, has caused the distruction of many hundreds of us . . . that our preservation depends on never loosing sight of this trait in their character, and being always prepared to meet it in whatever shape it may present itself."

Nearly two years of experience instructed Lewis as he wrote those lines, and he pointedly referred to generations of experience between whites and Indians—"the distruction of many hundreds of us." His commentary pulled in the hard core of a legacy of misunderstanding in the Encounter that often devolved to fear and hatred, even among enlightened observers. Precisely what ate at him so thoroughly when he wrote those lines we will never know. Nor will we understand what so bothered Alexander Ross when he warned that Indians, "even after years of friendly intercourse," would not change but would remain "morose, sullen, and unsociable" and could not "elevate himself to the habits of civilized men."

Ross' words document a cultural distance that can be ascribed to differences in living conditions, appearance, and even sexual customs. Those distances were real, and they kept whites and Indians looking across a cultural gulf. Did white traders see Indian families with understanding? Could Indians have conceived of the shape of white families' lives? Could Indians understand why Ross wondered how Indians could live "squatting, or lying amongst dirt and filth, dogs and fleas" rather than sitting in a chair in a house? The gulf was genuine, but within the circle of trade, where Indians and whites measured each other time and again, the gap also spreads open on a smaller issue. Europeans and Americans understood trade as a full-range activity in which nearly all things could be ascribed value and could be purchased. The conditions of the exchange could vary and the values could fluctuate, but the process itself had to be logical and predictable.

At the heart of the complaints that Ross and Lewis articulated was their objection to what they perceived as capricious behavior by their Indian trading partners. "Perfidy!" Ross declaimed, is the governing characteristic of Native Americans on the Columbia. But for those Indians who Ross castigated, trade was only *opportunity* to improve their lives, not the *context* of their lives. The Indians' world focused on relationships between themselves and their environment, between individuals in the group, and between them and the living spirits of their universe.

The Encounter on the Columbia, part of a great world-changing experience, spun a kaleidoscope of consequences that continue to inform us and shape our decisions in private and public matters. The Encounter changed this region, and it would never be as it was before. But in key respects the earliest sustained contact between Native Americans and whites on the Columbia changed the participants less than we might expect. Evaluations that whites and Indians made of each other, images individuals applied in general to members of the other culture, and the expectations each had of the other's behavior suggest that the Encounter encompassed a relatively narrow exchange between the "discovered" and the "discoverers."

The Encounter occurred too often at the sharpest and most circumscribed point of contact. Like a touching at the intersection of two swords, the trading exchange brought whole cultures together to engage in a bargain and a sale. Even a partial overlap of two circles of life, a wider encounter, had little chance. As the fur trade shriveled and allowed room for broader contacts between Native Americans and invading whites, Indians and whites learned more about their ways of living. The legacy, a child of revolutionary events, extended itself, continuing to leave its multicultural imprint on this Columbian world.

The Women of Fort Vancouver

by John A. Hussey

At dawn on March 19, 1825, a short, sturdy man strode across the courtyard of an unfinished log fort in the Oregon wilderness and smashed a bottle of rum against the flagstaff. "In behalf of the Honourable Hudson's Bay Company," he announced to a small gathering of British and French-Canadian fur traders and local Indians, "I hereby name this establishment Fort Vancouver."

The post thus christened by Governor George Simpson, chief executive officer of the larger part of the company's territories in North America, was situated on the north side of the Columbia River within the limits of the present city of Vancouver, Washington, nearly opposite the site of today's Portland. It became the headquarters and supply depot for the firm's vast Columbia Department, which extended from the Rocky Mountains to the Pacific Ocean, from Mexican California to Russian Alaska.

As far as company records have revealed, no women were present to join in the three cheers that followed the christening or to enjoy the "couple of Drams" distributed afterward to the assembled traders and natives. Even more than a year later, when the officer in charge of the post, Chief Factor John McLoughlin, made his annual report on conditions there, he noted the presence of only "two Women and two children on the Establishment."

In view of other evidence, however, we should not conclude that there were only two women at Fort Vancouver in 1826. Since the staff during the earliest years included a number of former employees of the North West Company, the great Montreal-based fur-trading firm that merged with the Hudson's Bay Company in 1821, almost cer-

tainly a sizable contingent of women lived at the fort practically from its beginning. The Nor'Westers were primarily French-Canadians, most of whom had formed "alliances" with the "daughters of the country." . . .

From the earliest days of bartering for furs along the eastern coast of North America, European traders had formed alliances with native women. Such unions were not merely the result of need for companionship and sexual fulfillment, although such motives were by no means absent. Rather, it was quickly found that barter was greatly facilitated among traders with native wives.

By marriage to the daughter of a chief or other prominent Indian, the European trader was often able to assure himself of the friendship and commerce of that man, his family, and his village, tribe, or group. Such a connection could sometimes also preserve the trader's scalp from unfriendly Indians. A native wife helped her husband learn the language of her group and kept him informed of local events related to his business. Equally important was the knowledge of wilderness lore among native women, particularly after the trade moved westward into regions where the Indians sometimes were not much interested in hunting for furs and where traders found it more profitable to become trappers themselves. A "daughter of the country" knew which berries and roots were edible. She could tan deer hides and make lodge coverings and clothing from them. She could fashion moccasins and snowshoes, items consumed in large quantities and essential for frontier travel. She was able to patch and gum canoes as well as make pack cords and saddlebags. She knew how to clean, dry, and pack furs. In addition to all

25

this, she performed the domestic chores of the household, both at the trading post and on the trail. The Indian wives of the fur traders often led hard lives, but the business of their husbands could hardly have operated as well without them.

Little is known of how these women felt about marriage to the Europeans, whether officers, voyageurs, or laborers. Apparently such unions were often welcomed by the women, largely because being the wife of an Indian was, among many groups, often still harder. Even though he might be a brute, a trader usually retained some respect for the notion that a wife was a companion and partner, not merely a piece of property. Alliance with a white man meant far greater security from such hazards as periodic starvation and intertribal warfare, and it promised easy access to such desired objects as metal utensils, beads, and jewelry. Above all, such unions brought increased status for the Indian woman and improved trade possibilities for her relations. Nor can mutual attraction be discounted. . . .

As with most Indian marriages, these unions could be dissolved by either party at any time. The trader, who might already be legally married in Canada or Europe, could leave his "country wife" with impunity as far as law was concerned. Since traders were shifted to distant posts with some regularity and since employment contracts eventually expired, such desertions were fairly frequent. The Hudson's Bay Company at times did not encourage employees to transfer their families with them, since moves were expensive. On occasion it was the wife who did not wish to leave her Indian family and her homeland.

Yet, within the culture of the fur trade, a union "in the fashion of the country" was generally not considered a mere temporary arrangement. Traders usually treated their women, as well as the women of their peers, as wives. As the mixed-blood children of these alliances grew up and as the daughters

in their turn married traders, a network of related families spread across British North America. Even more than Indian fathers, the traders were not disposed to give their daughters to men who would not protect them and provide for them. . . .

After the North West Company was merged into the Hudson's Bay Company in 1821, the fur trade of Canada largely became a monopoly extending from the Atlantic to the Pacific. Thus, it was no longer so important for traders to marry Indian women in order to help prevent the flow of furs to rivals. Also, the number of mixed-blood daughters had multiplied over the years, and the traders, especially officers and clerks, increasingly preferred them as mates. This decrease in the percentage of Indian consorts produced less immediate change in the structure of fur-trade society than might be imagined. Country marriages continued to be the rule for a number of years, particularly at the more isolated posts, and native and part-Indian wives lived in close proximity with little or no visible racial prejudice. . . .

Even when legal marriages became more widely available, however, a number of men refused them in the belief that years of living honorably together was evidence enough of legitimacy. In time, Canadian and British law sometimes took much the same view, to the disappointment of greedy white relatives who attempted to inherit the estates left to "country wives" and their children.

There were, of course, employees who did not consider themselves bound by company regulations over their domestic affairs or even by the requirements of decency. Men occasionally took wives despite the orders of their superiors, and sometimes they deserted their families under the cruelest circumstances. One case of abandonment that shocked even veteran traders occurred on the Columbia River in 1835. Chief Trader Francis Heron, an occasional visitor to Fort Vancouver, left Fort Colvile to go east on furlough, never to return. An employee described the scene as the express boat pulled away upstream: "On the beach stood his young halfbreed wife and babe in her arms both weeping. . . . The brute was as unconcerned at the parting . . . as if he was only taking a few hours excursion." At least one of his peers refused to speak to "old bloat" Heron forever afterward.

Another change . . . came in the early nineteenth century with the introduction of European women into the company's territories. A few adventurous white women had earlier attempted to join husbands or lovers at trading posts, and those efforts were seldom successful. But as more amenities became available at the larger establishments, it became practicable to think of bringing "lovely, tender exotics" from Scotland and England into the wilderness. . . .

The role of women at Fort Vancouver and the structure of family life and society there were basically determined by the long-established customs of the fur trade in general and by the rules, regulations, and practices of the Hudson's Bay Company in particular. The changes brought about by the rise of a mixed-blood population and the introduction of European wives were felt on the Columbia as well as in the other parts of the company's territories. Thus, the condition of women at the Columbia depot was not unique or even essentially different from that at other company posts across the continent. Yet, several factors existing at Fort Vancouver appear to have had a certain modifying influence on society there. Among these factors were the highly developed institution of slavery among the natives of the Pacific Northwest; the relatively large number of white female visitors and residents after the mid-1830s; and, most important of all, the prejudices, temperament, and humanity of Chief Factor John McLoughlin, who from 1825 to 1845 ruled the daily life at the post with a nearly absolute power that extended into the most minute details of domestic affairs.

Furthermore, the mere physical structure of the Columbia depot and its role as the administrative, agricultural, and supply center for a vast area of western North America resulted in a type of life matched at only a few of the company's larger posts. Fort Vancouver was a substantial establishment. At the peak of its development, about 1845, its log stockade enclosed an area as large as five football fields placed side by side. Within the pickets were twenty-two major buildings: large warehouses, a granary, a blacksmith shop, a bakery, apartments for officers and clerks, and dominating all, the French colonial-style Manager's Residence. Other workshops, barns, and dwellings for the servants extended over a wide area outside the palisade. Cultivated fields and grazing lands stretched for miles along the river and back into the woods. Not without reason did Narcissa Whitman call Fort Vancouver the "New York of the Pacific." . . .

The residents of Fort Vancouver thus had access to certain amenities and facilities—sawn lumber for houses, a school for their children, a chapel, a variety of purchasable clothing and manufactured goods—not often available at isolated stations. The presence of skilled artisans, farmers, and clergymen, as well as a constant stream of visitors, provided contacts with the outside world and with different sorts of people. Such influences gave life at the depot a certain cosmopolitan quality unknown at most company posts.

The standard of morality and the attitude toward women at the post were strongly influenced by the exemplary marital lives of Fort Vancouver's two chief personages, John McLoughlin and his longtime principal assistant and successor, James Douglas. While a youthful physician and clerk of the North West Company in the Great Lakes region, McLoughlin had married Marguerite McKay *á la façon du pays* ("in the fashion of the country") at Fort William. The bride was the daughter of a Swiss trader and an Indian or part-Indian woman. Marguerite McKay was nine years older than McLoughlin, and she had already borne four children as the result of her country marriage to Alexander McKay, a North West Company partner who had joined John Jacob Astor's Pacific Fur Company and was killed by Indians on the Northwest Coast in 1811. Why Marguerite and Alexander McKay separated is not known, but it is clear that she and McLoughlin were married before her first husband's death. She and two children accompanied the "Big Doctor" across the Rockies to the Columbia in 1824. . . .

When the Reverend Herbert Beaver, an Anglican clergyman appointed by the company as chaplain for the Columbia Department, arrived at Fort Vancouver in 1836, he quickly pronounced himself shocked by the "state of concubinage" in which the officers and servants lived, since to him a fur-trade marriage was no marriage at all. Beaver hoped to persuade McLoughlin to set a good example by becoming legally wed through a religious ceremony, but the "Big Doctor" never asked the chaplain to render such a service. The reasons for his refusal were several. For one thing, the chief factor and the clergyman were soon at loggerheads over a number of issues. McLoughlin was at that time becoming increasingly interested in the Roman Catholic church, and he had not wanted a Protestant chaplain at Fort Vancouver. But, more important, he apparently believed, as did James Douglas, that "the woman who is not sensible of violating any law, who lives chastely with the husband of her choice, in a state approved by friends and sanctioned by immemorable custom" was not to be condemned as immoral. In short, he probably saw no reason for disquieting his wife by insisting on a religious ceremony when she already considered herself adequately married.

Nevertheless, the insults hurled by the uncompromising Reverend Beaver must have had an effect. The "Big Doctor" and wife were soon quietly married (probably between 1836 and 1838) by James Douglas in his capacity as justice of the peace. . . .

Little information is available to show how the women of Fort Vancouver felt about these connections, regular or irregular. Most of them married, for the first time, at least, when very young. Sarah Ogden, daughter of Chief Trader Peter Skene Ogden, was only 14 when she married clerk Archibald McKinley in fur-trade fashion at Fort Vancouver in 1840. A clerk's daughter, not yet 16, was escorted from the depot to New Caledonia in 1837 to marry a man she had not seen for nearly four years. The Reverend Mr. Beaver said she was a "perfect automation" in the affair. It seems evident that, even among "gentlemen," marriages were sometimes matters negotiated between the would-be groom and the young woman's parents.

Still, romance surely entered into these connections as well. For example, 18-year-old Pierre Pepin reached Fort Vancouver as a newly recruited middleman and blacksmith in 1838. As was routine when brigades and expresses arrived, McLoughlin quartered the voyageurs and "pork eaters"—novice employees—among the servants in the village near the palisade. Pepin was assigned to the house of one Nancy Goodrich, Indian widow of a former occasional employee. Nancy's daughter, Susanne, was only a child at the time, and one of her feet had been so badly damaged in an accident that she had to walk with a stick. But Pepin must have been strongly attracted to her, because five years later, after he had freed himself from an unhallowed relationship, he returned and asked Susanne to marry him. When she expressed her willingness, Pepin approached her mother. Nancy Goodrich replied that if marriage was what Susanne wanted, it was fine with her, "only I live here with this girl, you'll have to keep me." It is recorded that the union of Susanne and Pierre Pepin was "long and congenial, though beset with poverty."

Little can be determined, from surviving post records, concerning the number of women who lived at Fort Vancouver. Generally, it was only some unusual circumstance, such as the granting of permission for an employee to take his family with him when traveling by boat, that brought the names of women into official documents. Thus, we must depend largely upon reminiscences, diaries, narratives of visitors, church records, and personal letters for what we know about the fort's resident women. In recent years, though, ethnological studies have shed additional light on the size and racial composition of the feminine population of the depot.

A reasonable estimate of the number of residents at Fort Vancouver in 1845, when the establishment was near its height of activity, is approximately 210 men, about 160 women, and perhaps 210 children, together with an unknown number of slaves of both sexes. The decline of Fort Vancouver began that same year when the main departmental depot was moved to Vancouver Island on the Northwest Coast.

The acquisition of the Oregon Country below the 49th parallel by the United States in 1846 and the discovery of gold in California two years later brought about a rapid, further reduction in the staff at Fort Vancouver. There were only about 14 officers and servants left in 1860 when the post was closed.

From marriage records it would appear that most of the female residents were Indians. One anthropologist has estimated that only about one in five was of mixed blood. A few European women lived at the fort from time to time, mostly for short periods. They formed such a small minority as to be numerically insignificant, but their social im-

pact was great. There were also, at times, several Hawaiian women living at Fort Vancouver.

The native women came from a variety of tribal backgrounds. About half of them were Chinooks, from groups living along the Columbia River from its mouth as far upstream as The Dalles. Apparently, proximity was as much a force in mate selection as it is today. The rest of the Indian wives were mostly from tribes situated along the coast and near inland posts such as Fort Walla Walla and Fort Colvile. A few were from distant points, such as a Shasta from California, a Stikine from Alaska, and a Nipissing from the Ontario/Great Lakes region.

Few of the Indian wives spoke French or English; thus, conversation between them and their husbands, and among the Indian wives themselves, was frequently in the Chinook Jargon, the simplified, eclectic language that facilitated trade in the Pacific Northwest. The mixed-blood women often learned French or English from their fathers and so had less difficulty talking with their husbands and European visitors. The prevailing tongue among the gentlemen's families appears to have been French.

Neither the language spoken nor skin color had much impact on the social and economic position of the individual woman. All depended on the rank of her husband. Chief factors, chief traders, clerks, chaplains, and—evidently at Fort Vancouver, at least—postmasters were considered "gentlemen" and were housed inside the pickets. Voyageurs, trappers, artisans, and laborers were classed as "servants" and lived inside the fort only if their duties required them to do so. Otherwise they lived outside the walls, in the village, on the farms, or at the mills.

By custom and regulation, these two classes were separate and distinct throughout the company's territories. Servants were not permitted to enter the quarters of the gentlemen for social reasons. Likewise, officers were cautioned against making frequent or prolonged visits to the dwellings of servants. . . .

Most of the families of the servants lived in 50 or 60 houses spread over the meadow west and southwest of the stockade. These village structures were built by the men themselves on Sundays and holidays, their only days off. They were generally small, one-story wooden affairs, sided with slabs from the company mill. Drawings show that some had an additional half story. A number were ceiled inside, and a few interiors were papered or plastered with clay. Archaeological excavations have revealed that many had dirt floors. . . .

Food preparation was done largely in native fashion. Each male employee received a weekly ration that varied with season and year. Governor Simpson noted that in 1841 the usual Saturday issue was 21 pounds of salted salmon and one bushel of potatoes, with occasionally a bit of venison or wildfowl. Two years later, McLoughlin wrote that three pounds of salted salmon and one and a half pounds of biscuit formed the "usual ration p. day," though when there were potatoes the allotment was "1 bushel p. week" of the latter. If preferred, each man could have instead one quart of "corn" and two ounces of "tallow" (lard) or three pounds of peas and two ounces of "tallow" per day. These amounts were intended to feed the men only, since rarely were rations provided for the families of servants. Although ample for one, the issue was monotonous, often disliked, and insufficient for a wife and several children.

One must conclude, therefore, that the wife not only prepared the food but had to supplement it as well. She could do so by taking to the woods and plains to gather edible roots and berries, as was the native custom. She could also earn credit at the sale shop by working for the company at such tasks as weeding crops and harvesting pota-

toes. Some women also earned credit or goods by acting as laundresses, nursemaids, or seamstresses for officers, clerks, and visitors.

Probably few women at Fort Vancouver went out themselves to forage for food or to perform mundane tasks. A high percentage of the women, particularly if they were Chinooks, owned one or more slaves. In 1837, an observer said there were plenty of slaves of both sexes in most households to "cut wood, hunt, and fish" and to perform "any extra work."

Another way the village wives contributed to the family income was by accompanying their husbands on trapping expeditions. The women were not paid directly for their arduous service, but they helped their men increase earnings by dressing and caring for the furs they captured. In addition to their salaries—generally £17 a year—company servants received four shillings each for one half of the "made Beaver" they produced after the "expenses of the hunt" were deducted. In addition to preparing pelts, the women and their slaves had to make and break camp almost daily, gather firewood, cook, dry meat and fish, take care of the children, patch clothing, dry furs and equipment after rains, and occasionally fight Indians beside their men.

For many years there were two main trapping and trading parties in the Columbia Department: the Snake Brigade, which operated largely in today's Inland Empire; and the Southern Brigade, which ranged through Oregon and, between 1829 and 1843, into California. Not all the men in these parties were based at Fort Vancouver, but many were. Records of both expeditions reveal how women contributed to the advancement of the trade. For example, in 1827 Peter Skene Ogden and his trappers were camped near the Rogue River. One day he watched the women at their tasks. "It is a pleasure," he wrote in his journal, "to observe the Ladys . . . vieing with each other who will produce on their return to Fort Vancouver the cleanest and best dress'd Beaver."

The journal kept by Chief Trader John Work during his expedition to California in 1832 and 1833 provides one of the best views of women on the trail. Work had not intended to bring his family with him on this journey. "I shall be very lonely without them," he told a friend, "but the cursed trip exposes them to too much hardship." But when the brigade left Vancouver his wife, Josette, and three young children, all girls, were along. As finally organized, the party consisted of 28 men, 22 women, 44 children, 6 Indians, and about 200 horses. They were destined to suffer bouts of severe illness, thirst, food poisoning, hunger, miserable weather, and—perhaps felt most keenly—a poor hunt. . . .

Wives of fort employees, whether they lived in the village or within the pickets, wore European clothing. The bolts of cloth available at the sale shop included such fabrics as bombazette, cassimere, and "fancy Earlston Ginghams;" such accessories as "Ladies short Kid Gloves," hooks and eyes, ribbons, "best diamond pins," "ladies round plated Hats," and shawls could also be had. Still, traces of native dress persisted. Almost universally the ladies, except for the few pure whites, retained the Indian leggin or gaiter, made of red and blue cloth richly ornamented with beads. The leggins were prominently displayed during horseback rides, when the women—again except for the Europeans—sat astride in Indian fashion. For most women the moccasin took the place of both shoes and stockings, but gentlemen's wives preferred European-style footwear. . . .

Child rearing provides another example of the cultural adjustment required of a native female trying to adapt to the ways of her white or mixed-blood husband. The men were universally firm on one point: they did not wish their offspring to be "disfigured" by having their heads flattened, as was the Chi-nook custom. Yet, for a Chinook woman to raise a round-headed child was considered a disgrace by her people, since in her society only slaves did not have their heads pressed in infancy. Some women felt it was so unbearable to have children marked as slaves that they are said to have resorted to abortion or infanticide.

In contrast to many of their sisters in the village, the wives of officers and clerks led lives of comparative ease. They were not required to cook or bake or perform most other household tasks. Company servants, all men, assumed such duties. Although these women did sew, care for their children, and wash the family's clothes, sometimes village women or Indians were hired even for these chores. Living quarters were supplied by the company. Most of the families of subordinate officers and clerks were housed in the long, 17-room dwelling known as the Bachelor's Quarters, but several other separate and semi-detached houses stood within the palisade, in addition to the Manager's Residence. . . .

Certainly, though, life for the women of the fort was not all loneliness, dullness, and inconvenience. Card parties and dances at the "Big House" were fairly frequent. On holidays and other days off, horseback rides and picnics provided entertainment. When an occasional naval vessel visited the depot, plays and athletic contests were put on, to which the women were invited.

Accounts by travelers provide glowing descriptions of the fine silver, the shining dinnerware, and the excellent and abundant food found in the mess hall. Undoubtedly, the families of McLoughlin and Douglas dined in comparable style in their private rooms, but the plight of the wives of the other officers and the clerks was quite different. Clerk Thomas Lowe complained bitterly that the "blackguard cook and steward" neglected and treated the families "in any way they thought proper." Although highly critical of almost everything at the fort, Herbert Beaver probably did not exaggerate much when he said that the meals prepared in the kitchen behind the "Big House" for the families of subordinates were "generally so badly cooked as to be uneatable." . . .

Concerns of a somewhat different nature preoccupied another small and ever-changing set of women at Fort Vancouver. These generally single women, whose employee husbands had died, deserted, or were ill or absent for long periods, were hard pressed to provide food and shelter for themselves and their children. The company generally encouraged unattached women at its establishments to move elsewhere, largely because they were an expense to the trade. Nevertheless, post managers sometimes found it impossible to enforce this policy, either because transportation was unavailable or because the officers—and the company—felt a sense of obligation toward women who had themselves performed outstanding service or whose husbands had served long and faithfully. And because some of these women simply had no other place to go, the company responded to their need. Thus, they were fed and housed, either within the stockade or in the village, according to the rank of their husbands. . . .

Changes at Fort Vancouver began soon after the arrival of the Whitman party of missionaries during September 1836. Since the group included two women, Narcissa Whitman and Eliza Spalding, McLoughlin could not continue his usual all-male hospitality, and he at once brought the entire party to the "Big House," introducing them to his wife and Mrs. Douglas. Because the women could not dine in the mess hall, the manager had the table in his sitting room enlarged, and Narcissa and Eliza ate there during the remainder of their stay, in the company of Mrs. McLoughlin, Mrs. Douglas, Eloisa McLoughlin, two of the fort's gentlemen, and, part of the time, Marcus Whitman and perhaps Henry Spalding. Mrs. Whitman and Mrs. Spalding were guests at the post for nearly two months in 1836 while their husbands were seeking sites for missions. . . .

Eloisa McLoughlin later maintained that the visit of the Whitman party began the breakdown of the isolation in which the fort women had lived. "Then we mingled more," she remembered. Journals and letters from subsequent years describe several instances of female visitors—and occasionally male guests as well—being entertained by the ladies of the "Big House." And when transient visitors were given housing in the Bachelors' Quarters, the families of the subordinate officers and clerks who lived there joined in similar social contacts. One Methodist missionary recalled that "the wives of the gentlemen, though they were native women and some half breeds, they used to come out and occupy the parlor with our ladies."

As time passed, it apparently became more and more usual to invite guests to participate in the picnics, horseback excursions, dances, and other entertainments that were regular features of life at the fort. Clearly, women were far less cloistered than they had been prior to 1836, but this relaxation had its limits. As far as post operations were concerned, the only known role of gentlemen's wives was to assist with the school. Evidently, they were not consulted on such domestic matters as the planning of menus or the selection and supervision of the cooks. These functions fell within the duties of the post surgeon. . . .

Part II
The Manipulated River

The spillway at Bonneville Dam
(Oregon Historical Society, ORHI 020807)

The Columbia Before It Was Tamed
How a Raging River Was Opened to Steamboat Traffic
by William D. Layman

In 1836, the steamship *Beaver* arrived in the Northwest. Built in England, she sailed around Cape Horn and up the Columbia to Fort Vancouver, where her engines were connected. Many working along the river were no doubt skeptical, but the *Beaver* soon proved itself a welcome successor to the broad-beamed bateaux which could only rely on strong paddling and favorable winds. Beginning in 1850, other steam-powered river craft were built, and soon there was reliable river transportation on the Columbia and tributaries such as the Willamette, the Lewis, and the Cowlitz rivers.

In 1858, steamers were successfully introduced on the stretches above Celilo Falls—but farther beyond the confluence of the Snake River there were severe problems.

Even so, the owners of the Oregon Steam Navigation Company as early as 1860 discussed the possibility of initiating steamer service above Priest Rapids, 400 miles south of the newly established border. However, little was known about the specifics of those waters. Early descriptions of the river were scarce, because many fur-trade journals went unpublished. The most reliable information sources available prior to 1860 were the maps of Captain Washington Hood (1838), Lieutenant Charles Wilkes (1841), and Governor Isaac Stevens (1853); and those sources suggested a number of serious obstructions upriver. In 1861, Captain John Mullan's map was published. It included the results of Captain Leonard White's survey of the upper Columbia the previous year. This survey delineated the course of the river in more accurate terms and identified additional stretches of fast water.... A detailed description of the various hazards, however, was unavailable until Lieutenant Thomas Symons made a remarkable reconnaissance trip downriver in September 1881.

Traveling in the bateau *Witchwater*, Symons made the descent from Kettle Falls to the mouth of the Snake River in 11 days. His landmark report on the river and its vicinity, published in 1882, brought increased recognition and interest in the resources of the region. The maps of that expedition, drawn by the talented Alfred Downing, gave congressmen and other interested parties the first close-up view of this major stretch of river. Symons fully believed the upper Columbia could be made navigable, but only at great expense. Even excluding a 35-mile boat railway around Grand Rapids and Kettle Falls, he estimated the costs of upper Columbia improvements at a staggering $3 million.

As predicted in Symons' report, pressures soon mounted for the Department of Army Corps of Engineers to make Priest Rapids passable. Leaders from the city of Ellensburg had told sternwheeler captain W. P. Gray in 1884 that they wanted boats to help ship the 500 tons of materials coming annually to their town over long, rough wagon roads. Moreover, the town's merchants wished to supply the 20 to 30 farmsteads in Wenatchee as well as the developing mining interests in the Okanogan country.

The next year, Congress responded by

allocating $6,000 for a detailed survey of Priest Rapids and Cabinet Rapids, 18 miles below Wenatchee. Yet, securing funds for surveying individual obstructions along the river was not favored by Major W. A. Jones, chief of engineers of the Military Department of the Columbia. In his annual report of 1886, Jones stated that it was perfectly obvious to him that projects for river improvements had to be guided by a comprehensive survey. He recommended spending $115,000 to provide a survey of 767 river miles of both the Snake and upper Columbia systems. Pressing for his recommendation, Jones concluded: "These are rivers of commanding importance, and it is quite time that they be studied by light of careful surveys such as are now in progress upon the Mississippi and Missouri rivers."

Persuasive as his arguments may have sounded, competition for Department of Army project dollars was extremely keen. The next funds granted for upper Columbia survey work were used to obtain a topographical survey of the next major obstruction, Rock Island Rapids, located 13 miles below Wenatchee. It was not until 1890 that Congress adopted a resolution involving any lengthy survey of upper Columbia waters. The 1890 plan allocated $70,000 for blasting channels and installing ringbolts at Priest, Cabinet, and Rock Island rapids. Ringbolts were embedded in rocks on shore. River craft attached lines to them and used winches to move upstream through swift water. This appropriation provided that up to $10,000 be spent to complete a survey from the international boundary to Rock Island Rapids, a distance of 294 miles.

By this time, Symons had returned to the Department of the Columbia with the new rank of captain. He selected assistant engineer William Cuthbert for the job, ordering him to begin fieldwork in March 1891 with the following assignment: first, to collect data for the topographical representation of the river and its immediate vicinity; second, to run accurate lines of levels to determine the river slopes; third, to determine the nature and extent of all obstructions to the free navigation of the river; and finally, to determine the character and amount of work necessary to secure a practicable navigation past these obstructions. . . .

Cuthbert's report generated nine large maps drawn by Downing. . . . Included in the report were profiles of the river and a large number of photographs taken to show its general character, with a particular emphasis on illustrating the bad stretches of water. Cuthbert conducted his fieldwork in two segments, and different photographers worked each of the sections. From the international boundary to the Spokane River, George Warren of Grayville, Illinois, took 71 photographs. From the Spokane River to the Okanogan River, O. C. Yocum, a surveyor from Mount Tabor, Oregon, took an additional 44 views. Forty of the total were selected to illustrate Symons' 1893 report to the chief of engineers. Prints of the entire series were also ordered in quintuplicate for the government exhibition at the 1892 Chicago World's Fair.

The field reports sent to Symons contained not only detailed descriptions of individual rapids, but other information as well. Commenting on population, Cuthbert stated, "Ten years ago [1881] you could count the white settlements on this part of the river on the fingers of one hand; now there are many settlements and small towns." Topographically, the river was described as flowing through a great canyon. Above the Spokane River, Cuthbert viewed the Columbia as well timbered with large amounts of beautiful and rich benchland along both sides. Below the Spokane, Cuthbert reported the timber disappearing and the canyon becoming much more rugged. The overall fall of the river between the Spokane and Okanogan rivers was recorded at 2.8 feet per mile. Nespelem

Canyon and Foster Creek Rapids, however, had a fall of between seven and eight feet per mile for three successive miles. Velocities of the current throughout the 214 miles surveyed averaged 3.5 miles per hour. Certain sections ran much faster, with Spokane Rapids the fastest at 15.38 miles per hour. Low water discharge was determined to be 50,000 feet per second, with a high water discharge of 300,000 feet per second. Such differentials in flow created tremendous seasonal fluctuations of water levels. Indeed, the high water marks seen in the photographs accompanying the report indicated a river of awesome power during spring runoffs.

. . . Cuthbert's survey reconfirmed what Symons had already come to believe: that the upper Columbia was unworthy of the great expenditures required to improve it. Cuthbert's estimate of improvement work was $18 million, considerably above Symons' earlier figure. In his view, there were too many disadvantages to the upper Columbia for it to become commercially important. Among them he listed the obstructions such as the Little Dalles, Kettle Falls, Grand Rapids, and Nespelem Canyon; the lesser rapids requiring auxiliary power; the generally swift and dangerous currents requiring great amounts of fuel in an area lacking adequate timber; and the topographic position of the river itself. "It must be remembered," he stated "that the Columbia flows through a great canyon or depression from 2,000 to 3,000 feet below the . . . country around it."

With such an unfavorable report, it was hardly surprising that upper Columbia River improvements authorized in 1894 were confined to the stretch between Wenatchee and Bridgeport. Yet, over the next 15 years, a tremendous influx of immigrants settled the choicest upriver farmlands, increasing demands for sternwheeler services. An opportunity presented itself in 1905 when an updated survey between Wenatchee and Kettle Falls was authorized, but the Seattle District

Corps of Engineers chief, Lieutenant Colonel John Millis, instructed his assistant to survey no farther than Bridgeport. This was bad news to farmers who had planted orchards on the rich Columbia bottomlands above Bridgeport. However, three influential figures responded to their plight. They were Dr. N. G. Blalock, director of the Open Waters Association of Washington State; Professor W. D. Lyman of Walla Walla; and Fred McDermott, veteran upper Columbia sternwheeler captain. Speaking to commercial clubs along the river, these men mounted a strong campaign to open the Columbia from the Canadian border to the Pacific Ocean.

By the end of 1907, a two-pronged strategy was devised: to seek state aid for river improvements and to lobby the Corps of Engineers to authorize a new survey above Bridgeport. In December, the latter was approved; and by January 1908, four river captains under McDermott's leadership took Seattle district assistant engineer Eugene Ricksecker and Wenatchee photographer B.C. Collier upriver as far as Grand Rapids in the steamer *Enterprise*. Ricksecker, although describing the trip as unbearably cold, reported the project worthy of funding. Two months later, the new district chief, Major Hiram M. Chittenden, recommended allocating $175,000 to open this section of river to steamboat navigation.

It was the state of Washington . . . that took legislative action. In March 1909, a measure was passed to authorize $50,000 for channel improvement work above Bridgeport and to establish the Columbia River Improvement Commission. McDermott, understandably elated at this victory, not only headed the commission but took charge of the work. In November 1909, he piloted the newly acquired sternwheeler *Yakima* upstream to Foster Creek Rapids. Within days, the first dynamite blasts were felt 25 miles away on the Big Bend of the Columbia Plateau.

Such action by the state of Washington was unprecedented. Congress responded in June 1910 by authorizing $100,000 to continue the effort as outlined in Chittenden's 1908 report. For the next six years, government crews worked the stretch of river between Bridgeport and Grand Rapids. Finally, after another $100,000 had been expended, the Corps deemed the project completed. The goal of furnishing a reasonably safe outlet for the products of this rich and productive country was attained.

In retrospect, Symons was probably correct. While vitally important to some, commerce above Bridgeport never really thrived. For three years, from 1911 to 1914, McDermott managed a business along the Columbia from the town of Lincoln upstream to Kettle Falls. He then moved downstream to Pateros; and although he made occasional runs above Box Canyon well into the 1920s, his main business was conducted between Pateros and Bridgeport. Ironically, the demise of river transportation had been set in motion much earlier, when locomotives entered the West. After the rail lines were installed along northern Washington rivers, the boilers of the sternwheelers grew cold.

The 214-mile stretch of river between the mouth of the Okanogan and the international boundary formed an exciting part of the Columbia's great journey to the Pacific. Its rapids held awe and fascination for those who dared run them, be they adventurous fur traders or boatmen traveling up- and downriver under steam power. The Cuthbert survey and records left by Fred McDermott possess a value in our time not previously imagined by those who saw the river with navigation in mind. It is fortunate that such men wishing to alter the character of the upper Columbia through "river improvements" succeeded in giving future generations such a clear and lively record of its original character. Particularly, the maps and photographs serve the vital function of helping us remember the upper Columbia as it was.

In this century, the three reservoirs behind Wells, Chief Joseph, and Grand Coulee dams have inundated the former banks of the river. It is only with great imagination that one can sense the free-flowing river there at all. . . . We see the wild river described in the narratives of Thompson, Ross, David Douglas, John Work, and others. We know better the waters that were a life source for generations of native peoples.

Engineering the Cascades Canal and Locks, 1876-1896

by William F. Willingham

The early growth and development of the Oregon Country depended on the effective use of the region's major waterways. These rivers served as highways for steamboat transport of agricultural produce and mineral wealth from the backcountry to Portland. . . .

In their natural state, the Columbia and Willamette rivers presented numerous obstacles to easy navigation, even for light-draft steamboats. Rapids, rocky reefs, and shoals encumbered the Columbia; snags, shifting channels, and heavy sedimentation caused by annual freshets clogged the Willamette. . . . Surmounting this blockage ultimately required building a canal and locks. Such a major project called for the expertise and financial support of the national government.

The United States Army Corps of Engineers supplied the needed federal assistance, for Congress had charged the Corps of Engineers with carrying out the federal government's constitutionally mandated responsibility for improving the nation's navigable waterways.

The story of the Cascades Canal and Locks presents a case study of how federally sponsored transportation improvements helped develop the West after the Civil War. It also demonstrates one aspect of how the Army Corps of Engineers assisted the economic growth of the Pacific Northwest in the last third of the nineteenth century.

Commercial interests in Portland were determined to make the most of the city's location. Situated 10 miles above the confluence of the Willamette and Columbia rivers and 108 miles above the mouth of the Columbia, the city owed its existence and early prominence to its river site. Strategically situated in a region rich in natural and agricultural resources, the city's growth and prosperity seemed preordained. . . .

The *continued* growth and prosperity of Portland, however, clearly depended upon river improvements. . . . The immediate impetus for river transportation improvements arose from the discovery of gold in eastern Oregon and Idaho in the 1860s and the subsequent recognition that the Columbia Plateau was well suited to large-scale dryland wheat farming.

In response to lobbying for Portland interests, the newly established Pacific office of the Corps of Engineers, located in San Francisco, began Oregon operations in 1867. Early work on the Columbia above Portland involved survey and rock removal from the river channel. Captain John C. Ainsworth, president of the Oregon Steam Navigation Company (OSN), directed the Corps' attention to the most dangerous rapids between Celilo and Priest Rapids, a distance of 200 miles. . . .

Ainsworth expressed particular concern over the Umatilla, Homly, and John Day rapids. In low water, many boats ran on the rocks at these obstructions. Boat crews were forced to guide their craft through the rapids by means of lines extended to the shore. Even with these precautions, only the very shallow-draft riverboats could operate during low-water periods, and these steamers proved wholly inadequate for the quantities of grain needing shipment. . . .

Open river improvements had limited value as long as the obstructions at the Cascades and The Dalles remained. At these two locations, the entire force of the river was compressed within a space of less than 200 feet. The boulder-choked rapids and precipitous fall of the contracted river completely blocked navigation at these points. From the days when traffic on the river first appeared, means had to be devised to transport people and goods past the barrier presented by Cascade Rapids. The earliest methods consisted of a one-mule outfit built in 1851 and placed in operation at the Washington Territory side of the river. For 75 cents, 100 pounds of "emigrant effects" could be portaged safely around the rapids. Mules and cars added by subsequent owners improved the service somewhat. Eventually, a competitor became active on the Oregon side of the river.

In 1862, the OSN gained control of the portage roads, mules, and cars on the Oregon side. By adding ownership of portage facilities to their existing domination of boat traffic, the OSN obtained a secure monopoly of activity on the river. A steam locomotive—the first in Oregon—and several cars replaced the mules. River travelers enjoyed an efficient and quick portage on five miles of steel rail. The OSN located a similar operation, over twice as long, as Celilo Falls.

The blockage of the Cascades, about 45 miles east of Portland, extended for 4.5 miles. The lower 4 miles of the congested river channel contained eddies, boulders, and rocky reefs, with a fall of 12 feet at low water. The upper half mile possessed the worst rapids, with a low-water fall of 24 feet. The swift current further complicated navigation. In addition, the yearly summer runoff caused a rise of between 25 and 60 feet above low water in the rapids below the Cascades. The difference in the slope of the surface at high water was never less than 14 feet for all flood stages. These factors complicated the problem of improvement for navigation.

Recognizing the importance of the obstruction on the Columbia River at the Cascades, the Corps performed a preliminary survey in 1874 and a more thorough one in 1876. Based on these studies, the Corps proposed a canal and locks for the worst rapids and removal of the most dangerous reefs and rocks in the river below. Moreover, the Corps also concluded that a canal would be necessary at The Dalles. A board of engineers for the Pacific Coast, acknowledging the monopoly enjoyed by the OSN on the Columbia, stated in 1878 that "the whole of the navigation of the Upper Columbia and Snake rivers is now in the hands of a single company. . . . The only way to throw the entire river open to competitive navigation will be by the construction of a canal at The Dalles as well at the Cascades."

Senator John H. Mitchell described the situation more dramatically in a Senate speech: "Never in the history of this or any other country was any natural highway, much less one of the grand proportions of the great Columbia, held so exclusively, so mercilessly, and so regardlessly of the rights of the people in the control of unyielding corporate rapacity and power as is that of the Columbia. . . . It [OSN] defies competition; it preys upon the producers of Oregon, Washington, and Idaho with a relentless hand; and its exchequer overflows with revenues wrung from the people of the great Northwest, through unreasonable and unconscionable freight and passenger exactions."

Acceding to rising demands that the OSN monopoly be broken and accepting the Corps' preliminary survey and plan of 1874, Congress appropriated $90,000 in 1876 for final planning and initial construction of the Cascades Canal.

The Portland engineer officer in charge, Major John Wilson, then received permission to hire an engineer expert in canal work. After an extensive nationwide search, he selected Channing M. Bolton to supervise the planning and building of the Cascades Canal. . . . By February 1877, Wilson presented his plan for the construction of a canal and locks around the Cascades, at a cost of $1,188,680. As modified by the board of engineers for the Pacific Coast and the chief of engineers, the plan called for a canal 8 feet deep, 50 feet wide, and 7,200 feet long at low water, with two locks, each 8 by 70 by 300 feet at low water. A guard gate at the upper end of the canal would be used when repairs were necessary or during extreme high-water periods. The work changes increased the project costs to $1.7 million. . . .

Complicated land condemnation proceedings necessary to acquire property for the Cascades Canal and Locks delayed work until November 1878. In October 1877, Major Wilson informed the OSN, owners of the proposed canal site, that the government needed 47.32 acres for the project. The company offered to sell at $200 per acre, with a reservation for a railroad right-of-way across the property. The Secretary of War rejected the reservation and ordered Wilson to begin condemnation proceedings. After lengthy negotiations, the Corps agreed to reduce its request by 4.45 acres and the company dropped its demand for a right-of-way. In addition, OSN offered the Corps permanent access through its property to a county road and use of a house by the engineers during construction. New complications arose, however, when another company claimed ownership of the property under negotiation. Because of the clouded title and a belief that the OSN proposal was too expensive, the Secretary of War decided in February 1878 to proceed with the condemnation. The matter came to trial in July, and the jury valued the land at $7,500. Title passed to the Corps on October 5, 1878.

Shortly before his transfer from the Portland Engineer Office in October 1878, Major Wilson awarded the contract for the initial excavation to a New York firm, Ball and Platt. . . .

Only two months after work had commenced, A. H. Ball, senior partner and managing contractor, died from exposure while supervising construction. For several months thereafter, little was accomplished for lack of competent supervisory personnel within the company and because of delays in receiving and assembling construction equipment. Severe weather conditions at the site also slowed work. High winds and large masses of floating ice prevented transportation on the river and isolated the Cascades labor force for days at a time during December. In addition, heavy rains and high water plagued the excavation work throughout the winter and spring; rainfall for the period between February and June totaled 57.28 inches. As construction limped along, primitive living conditions at the canal site worsened matters. Substandard housing led to low worker morale, and the lack of nearby medical facilities made difficult the provision of proper care for injured workers. When a collapsing derrick "terribly" gashed one of the laborers across the face, Assistant Engineer Bolton reported that he used a sewing needle and ordinary silk thread to close the man's cut.

. . . The labor force, never adequate according to Gillespie. . . . struck for higher pay and complained about the use of Chinese workers on the project. Actually, if anyone had grounds for complaint, it was the 100 Chinese; for they were paid 85 cents a day, compared to $1.75 earned by white laborers. While refusing to increase wages, Major Gillespie alleviated the labor problems by paying workers as if they were government employees, from the funds due the contractor. He used the same procedure in the purchase of materials. Finally, to top off Gillespie's difficulties, his chief assistant on the canal, Channing Bolton, resigned in May 1879.

Based on Gillespie's repeated complaints that the contractor had failed to prosecute the work effectively, the chief of engineers, with the approval of the Secretary of War, ordered the contract abrogated on November 12, 1879. The contractors vacated the site on January 2, 1880, and the government purchased their equipment and other material at an appraised price in March 1880. In the meantime, work had resumed under the Corps' direct supervision. . . .

As a result of this experience, much of the work on the canal and locks subsequently was done by hired labor with materials purchased by bid on the open market. All management for the project came under the direct supervision of civilian assistant engineers or officers of the Corps. The Corps let contracts for specific tasks only, such as wharf construction or open river rock removal; general responsibility stayed with the Corps of Engineers.

After the government assumed full authority, it built better housing for workers and supplied room and board for $3.75 per week. The Corps also set up a dispensary and hired a resident doctor at $100 a month. White laborers on the project received, depending on their skills, from $2 to $4.50 a day. Top pay went to the civilian assistant engineer in charge; his salary came to $175 a month. Before 1891 yearly peak employment rarely exceeded 200 workers. Lieutenant Charles Powell had local charge of the project from October 1878 until his promotion to Portland engineer officer in July 1881. Lieutenants Philip Price, Willard Young, Edward Burr, and Harry Taylor succeeded Powell in local charge of operations until the canal opened in 1896.

The town of Cascade Locks also developed as a result of the canal project. As early as 1880 the community growing next to the canal work site included about 100 permanent residents and 350 transient workers. The emergence of a fishing industry in the vicinity of Cascade Locks aided the gradual growth of the town and the surrounding area in the late nineteenth century. The scenic beauty of the Columbia River Gorge also attracted a summer tourist trade from Portland. By 1900, there were about 550 people living in Cascade Locks and the immediate vicinity. . . .

When finally completed, the canal had the capacity to handle traffic at any stage of the river up to 42 feet above low water. This capability was the result of a project modification made in 1894: by adding a concrete floor and side walls, that part of the canal between the upper gates of the lock and the upper guard gate could function as a second lock. In 1886, the chief of engineers approved a proposal to enlarge the gate span to the same 90-foot width as the lock. Two years later, the engineers gained approval to build the gates of steel rather than wood after discovering that suitable wood of the necessary dimensions was scarce and of questionable durability. The final addition, a movable wall-gate device above the upper lock gates, ensured against failure of the main lock. It was rarely used. . . .

. . . Work slowed at the canal lock site in 1881 as concentration focused on improvements to the river approaches below the canal. Since the exact placement and reference dimensions of the lock and canal depended upon the regiment of the river at low water, the removal of great quantities of rock and reefs in the river below the canal became essential. This involved dangerous, arduous work in which seven workers lost their lives. Again, after initial unsatisfactory work by contractors, the Corps completed the river improvements with hired labor under its own supervision. In a comparative test, the engineers found that hired labor removed twice the rock at one-half the price over private contractors. The approach work consumed five years and $116,519; the original project cost estimate now tripled to over $3,623,000. Full work resumed at the canal site proper in 1886, and ten years were necessary to bring the project to the stage where the canal could be opened to traffic. To assist river shippers until the canal opened, the Corps allowed the state to build and operate a portage railroad across the canal grounds after 1891. . . .

The magnitude of the work stands out clearly in the following construction and materials statistics, expressed in cubic yards:

Earth and rock excavation	817,825
Concrete	93,275
Stone masonry	85,491
Slope pavement	117,852

The project also required 3.3 million pounds of iron and steel for the gates, anchorages, values, and other items. . . .

Captain Philip Price, resident engineer in 1883, reported that because of high water no work could be done from the middle of May to the middle of August. Unfortunately, this was also the driest and hence most favorable time for work at the site; during the remainder of the year, when low water permitted work in the canal, excessive rainfall and frequent snowstorms hampered the laborers. The average annual rainfall came to 78 inches; and in the winters of 1884-85 and 1889-90, 8 and 12 feet of snow, respectively, covered the Cascades locale. During the wet season, the men had to labor in heavy oilskin coats and awkward rubber boots. Price explained that men so encumbered could produce only about half their normal work. He noted that the canal site was "exceedingly rough and broken, covered with a mass of boulders, varying from one-half to one hundred tons and more in weight." Once lifted by derricks, tramways with mule-drawn cars removed the excavated material. The vast quantities of water and mud prevented the use of wagons or carts. . . .

By 1888, the engineers had finished only about a third of the work on the Cascades Canal, and local public pressure to complete it reached a peak. The annual meetings of the Columbia Waterway Convention, an association of commercial interests and farmers, passed resolutions imploring Congress to appropriate funds to complete the Cascades Canal quickly and to begin similar work at The Dalles. Senator John Mitchell delivered speeches demanding that Congress act, and newspaper editors issued clarion calls for larger appropriations and more expeditious construction.

A shortage of funds and transfers of responsibility for the project caused a complete suspension of work for several months in 1886, in 1888, and again in 1890. Congress made no appropriations at all for the canal in 1877, 1883, 1885, 1887, 1889, and 1891. The average yearly amount funded constituted only a fifth of what the engineers in charge stated could have been profitably expended. In obvious frustration, Major Thomas Handbury wrote in his annual report for 1888 that small appropriations parceled out over 12 years had caused nothing but problems. "At this rate," he observed, "it will require perhaps twenty-four years more before any benefit to commerce will result from this work, or the country receive the least renumeration for the month expended." Echoing the local folk wisdom, he noted that "a generation will have been born and gone to its grave between the beginning and the ending of an enterprise which a healthy syndicate would have prosecuted to completion within six years at farthest after commencement, and been in the enjoyment the balance of time of a liberal income from the money invested."

Not fully aware of the numerous difficulties encountered by the Corps of Engineers, the public and politicians accused the Corps of mismanaging the project. In particular, public outrage centered on the use of hired labor under Corps supervision. Congressman Binger Hermann of Oregon and various state newspapers asserted that private enterprise could do the work faster and more economically under the contract system, ignoring the original unsatisfactory results of contract work for excavation and river improvements. *The Dalles Daily Chronicle* complained that "money may come and go, appropriations be made and squandered, but the yawning chasm at the Cascades gaps to heaven in vain, for the near waters of the Columbia. . . . There is no hope of change until the work is taken from the war department and turned over to contractors."

In a lengthy defense of the Corps' management of the Cascades Canal project, Major Handbury forcefully presented his view. He asserted that the government was "honestly and economically" building the canal with its own plant and work force. He rhetorically asked: "Shall these officers, whose ability, zeal, and integrity can not be doubted, be pushed aside and the management of this work be turned over to an individual whose only merit may be that he thinks he can do it cheaper and is willing to give bonds?" Handbury had little regard for contractors, as he felt dishonest ones would seize every opportunity "for increasing his profits by slighting his work and using poor and cheap material." He added that "even the honest one will be often sorely tempted to straining a point here and there in spite of every precaution that can be taken." How else, Handbury concluded, could a contractor profit, since he "could not be permitted in any way to change the plans of the work but would be required to carry these out according to specifications given him in minute detail."

In sum, Handbury stated: "I am of the opinion that it would be detrimental to the work and to the interests of the Government to attempt its completion by contract; and urgently recommend that the full amounts that can be profitably expended each year as recommended by the Chief of Engineers be made available, and that the work be prosecuted by hired labor with the plant belonging to the Government."

Congress rejected Handbury's advice. The River and Harbor Act of July 13, 1892, specified that the appropriation for the Cascades Canal be expended by a continuing contract. Congress did materially increase the appropriations, however, voting $326,250 in 1892 and $1,239,653 in 1893. Specifications for completing the entire project were put to bid, and the J. G. & I. N. Day Company of San Francisco received the contract on January 31, 1893. . . .

Unfavorable weather and contractor delays necessitated three contract extensions of a year each. The record flood of 1894 damaged the lower end of the canal and required such repairs as raising the heights of the canal walls and strengthening the revetment work. In addition, District Engineer Major James Post and a board of engineers concurred in recommending the creation of a second lock adjoining the first by constructing walls between the upper lock gate and the upper guard gate; in this way, the canal would be navigable to all stages up to 42 feet above low water. The proposed modifications added $318,573 to the ultimate cost of the project and were not completed until 1914. Despite the delays and modifications, the large appropriations enabled the Corps to open the unfinished canal in 1896. To that date, $3,793,496.94 had been expended on the project.

Oregonians greeted the opening of the canal with great excitement and celebration. On November 5, 1896, several hundred excursionists passed through the locks on steamboats to view the great work at close quarters. The steamer *Sarah Dixon* had a small cannon bolted to her deck, and at appropriate intervals she fired booming salutes. And well she might, for the Cascades Canal's construction had been a formidable task, requiring many novel engineering details. As Major Walter Fisk, Portland district engineer, noted at the dedication ceremonies at The Dalles, "only those who have been engaged on the work can realize its magnitude." . . .

The benefits to commerce came immediately. In 1895, the last year of its operation, the state portage railway had moved 8,122 tons of freight; but the canal carried many times that amount annually at no charge to any shipper, commercial or otherwise. The value of freight through the canal in most years between 1898 and 1920 equaled the entire cost of constructing the project. In addition, the canal restored a competitive balance to freighting. The Union Pacific Railroad, which had replaced the OSN as the sole carrier along the Columbia, now had competition from river shippers. By making the shipment of bulk materials on the river more economical, the canal helped moderate railroad rates.

The Cascades Canal and Locks also provided experience valuable in the effort to build a canal and locks around the obstructions above The Dalles. When the Corps of Engineers completed that undertaking in 1915, open river navigation on the Columbia extended from Astoria, Oregon, to Lewiston, Idaho, a distance of 700 miles. In building the Cascades Canal, the Corps of Engineers expended the transportation facilities essential to the economic development of the inland Pacific Northwest in the late nineteenth and early twentieth centuries. The canal faithfully served its role until drowned out in 938 by the backwater of the Bonneville Dam.

Wheat Sacks Out to Sea
The Early Export Trade from the Walla Walla Country
by Donald W. Meinig

The Columbia Basin wheat country has been one of the world's most important grain export regions for nearly three-quarters of a century. Located more than 2,000 miles from the major domestic market area, with the grain regions of the Central Plains intervening, the farmers of the Walla Walla, Palouse, Big Bend, and other sections have been critically dependent upon a foreign outlet for their crops. Nevertheless, the existence of overseas markets had not been the original impetus of agricultural colonization in this area, and the development of this modern orientation marked a new era in the regional economy and was, in many ways, an achievement as difficult as it was important.

Permanent settlement in this "Interior" of the old Oregon Country was but ten years old when, in 1868, a British vessel embarked from Portland with a full cargo of wheat for Liverpool. The first colonists had been attracted to the Walla Walla Valley by the mining boom which followed upon a series of gold discoveries in the peripheral mountain districts. Nearly all came as stockmen, for whereas this extensive area of rolling bunchgrass prairie was obviously a rich grazing domain, there had been widespread agreement for many years that agriculture would undoubtedly be severely limited to the well-watered valleys. Despite rapidly mounting demands for flour and feed, grain cultivation expanded slowly at first while the pioneers, through trial and error, tested the environment with a variety of crops and farming practices.

Beginning in the middle 1860s, settlers came to realize that the hill lands, hitherto thought wholly unsuited to cultivation, were in fact magnificent wheat soils. This discovery enormously enlarged the agricultural potential of the Interior and accelerated the influx of settlers. Meanwhile, an increasing amount of wheat and oats was being produced in the mountain valleys nearer to the mining districts; and as the mining boom leveled off and the production of the Interior continued to increase, it became apparent that some other outlet had to be found to sustain the expansion of the farming frontier.

Downriver shipments began in 1867. In the spring of that year, Walla Walla flour was introduced and successfully competed with Willamette flour at Umatilla and The Dalles. This development, however, was but a broadening of the original market, as these centers were chiefly serving the Boise Basin and John Day mining trade. It was not until June that an important change was indicated, when word was received that 1,000 barrels had been shipped to San Francisco at a profit. The volume of downriver movements now rapidly increased; a reorientation took place, and with the establishment of the direct tie between Portland and Liverpool in the following year, a new economic life line for the Columbia Basin was created.

For convenience of examination, this 16,000-mile market connection may be divided into three sections: from the farms to the landings on the Columbia and Snake

46

rivers; the downriver route to Portland; and the ocean voyage from Portland to Liverpool. Each of these segments had its distinctive marketing features and problems which taxed the ingenuity, the patience, and the pocketbooks of Walla Walla citizens for many years.

The produce of the Walla Walla Valley had to be hauled 32 miles overland to Wallula on the Columbia. As early as 1862 the exorbitant rates charged by the teamsters had prompted a group of local businessmen to obtain a charter to build a railroad to the landing. No rails were ever laid by this company, however, and agitation for a line continued unabated. Whether it was the success of the downriver flour shipments that prompted a renewed attempt is not wholly clear, but in December 1868, Dr. Dorsey S. Baker incorporated the Walla Walla and Columbia River Railroad Company. Financial difficulties delayed construction, but grading was commenced in 1872. The first section of 16 miles from Wallula to Touchet was opened for traffic on March 25, 1874, and the line was completed to Walla Walla on October 30, 1875.

This little narrow-gauge railroad immediately did a flourishing business and was an important stimulus to the growth of settlement. However, the direction of expansion was northeastward into the valleys along the margins of the Blue Mountains, farther and farther from the terminus. For the settlers who spread over the divide into the Touchet and Pataha valleys, the railroad was too distant for profitable shipment. Dayton farmers had to ship their grain over the steep grades to the Tucannon, thence down that canyon to the wheat landing and warehouse at Grange City on the Snake River; farmers in the Pataha area had an equally difficult haul to New York Bar, the nearest accessible river point. As the frontier pushed farther eastward, transportation became even more difficult, for the river could be reached only by tortu-

ous roads winding down 2,000 feet from the canyon rim. Randall Mills has well described the problems of the farmers using these roads: "Onto heavy wagons the wheat would be stacked; then the driver, perched on a seat high on the sacks would yell at the long string of horses and start them on their way. Mile after mile, usually part of a procession of farm wagons, he would trundle along, the sweat eroding channels through the dust that settled on his face. But when he came to the river . . . he had another long trip, practically straight down. . . . The road twisted and wound down, down, down, and a loaded wagon had to drag logs, be snubbed, and be held back with ropes all the way from the crest to the landing. A trip or two up and down one of those roads left a farmer exhausted and his vocabulary of cussing pumped dry."

Along with sweating and swearing there was also considerable thinking about some alternative: instead of fighting gravity all the way down, why not let gravity do the work? In 1879, a wooden pipe was constructed, 4 inches square and 3,200 feet long, from the canyon rim to the river landing. In the first trials, gravity overdid the job; the kernels descended with such speed that they were ground into coarse flour and soon cut holes in the pipe. The chute was therefore rebuilt with a series of upturns every 100 feet to decrease the velocity and this time worked so well that within a few years several others were constructed. Pendleton, Dayton, and Pomeroy achieved railroad connections by 1886, but in the eastern Walla Walla and adjacent Palouse countries farmers continued for many years to haul by wagon to the landings or grain chutes.

Getting the wheat to the landings was but the initial difficulty, for river transportation was also beset with many problems. In 1875, only two boats with a combined capacity of 250 tons were attempting to handle the traffic from Wallula, and although the number and the size of the boats was increased in later years, they were rarely able to move the harvest in proper time. . . .

Yet, the most serious problems were downriver, where Columbia navigation was completely blocked in two places. The upper barrier consisted of four major obstacles along a distance of 13 miles, where nature had "with unmerciful and unsparing hand . . . placed an absolute embargo on navigation": Celilo Falls, a drop of 20 feet at low water; Ten-Mile Rapids; The Dalles, where "the passage is so narrow that the river is polarized, as it were, and set on edge . . . and, the waters are dammed up at the head until the slope becomes such as to produce an enormous velocity"; and Three-Mile Rapids. The lower barrier was the Cascades, four miles of exposed rocks, shoals, and rapid water. No boat could possibly move upstream over these obstacles, and although several empty of cargo were taken down, this was done only at the risk of complete loss. These features divided the Columbia into three segments, commonly referred to as the Upper River (from Priest Rapids and Asotin to Celilo), the Middle River (from The Dalles to the Cascades), and the Lower River (from the Cascades to the Pacific).

During the mining boom of the 1860s portage railroads were constructed around these barriers, but the service was slow and the charges high, and a means of achieving uninterrupted navigation continued to be a lively topic throughout the Interior for decades. Canal and lock systems were proposed very early, but surveys indicated that the costs would be enormous. Others suggested that bulk grain might be carried directly to Portland on barges built sufficiently sturdy to withstand the passage over the falls and rapids, but apparently none were ever built. For a time, there was great interest in the proposal for boat railways, by which the flatbottomed sternwheelers could be hauled overland around Celilo Falls and The Dalles.

Detailed surveys were made, and elaborate plans were drawn for 42-wheeled carriages that were to be pulled along a track 25-1/2 feet wide by cables attached to a stationary steam engine. Although recommended by several government engineers and receiving the enthusiastic support of many local citizens, such structures were never built. By the 1880s, the dredging of some of the rapids was the only river improvement completed.

The regional promotion writers of the day were wont to describe the Columbia as a "majestic, broad highway to the mighty Pacific"; as far as the farmers were concerned, a traveler of 1880 painted a more realistic picture: "To give an accurate idea of the trouble of transportation from Walla Walla to the ocean, we will follow a sack of wheat from the field where it is grown. It is hauled to the depot at Walla Walla and there stored, to await its turn when the twenty-five thousand tons already ahead are taken away. Then it is put upon the cars and taken to Wallula; then it is put upon the boat and taken to Umatilla and transferred to another boat for Celilo; then it goes through the warehouse to the cars, taken to The Dalles and stored again; then it goes by boat to the Upper Cascades, and is then delivered to the railroad, by which it is taken to the Lower Cascades and transferred to another boat, by which it is taken up the Willamette to Portland. Here again it is stored, and thence sent down the river to Astoria and the ocean."

Aside from the change at Umatilla, which was made only during very low water stages, in the journey from the farm to the ocean vessels, the wheat was handled seven times at transshipment points and accrued storage costs in four warehouses. As the same writer concluded, "fortunes are being made slowly there now in wheat culture, with all the disadvantage of the isolated situation and an imperfect transportation." During this time, wheat normally sold in Portland for twice the sale price at Walla Walla, the cost of transportation equalling that received by the farmers: adequate justification for the attention given to transport problems which permeates the literature of that day.

In 1882, the Oregon Railway & Navigation Company completed its rail line along the south bank of the Columbia from Wallula to Portland. River service from Celilo to Ainsworth, at the junction of the Columbia and Snake rivers, was withdrawn, the portage railroad around The Dalles was abandoned, and that at the Cascades was little used. The O.R.& N. also obtained a lease on the Walla Walla and Columbia River Railroad and widened it to standard gauge, thus giving Walla Walla a through connection with Portland. Yet, this by no means solved the export problems of the Interior; indeed, the building of this line actually intensified the agitation for navigation improvement, for there was no government regulation of transportation in this era, and only competition could bring a reduction in freight rates. No competing river service could exist as long as the Columbia navigation barriers remained, for the O.R.&N. controlled the portages and, with their rail line, could lower rates temporarily to drive a competitor from business. The "Columbia River Pass," therefore, continued to be the focal point of agitation....

This monopolistic control by the O.R.&N. brought it some excellent profits as well as some eloquent abuse. The Honorable John Mitchell, senator from Oregon, undoubtedly expressed the sentiments of many of the local citizens with this rather spirited denunciation: "the Columbia River being the only real pass through which the productions of the Great Columbia Basin or inland empire can find their way to the seaboard, it has been made possible for one corporation engaged in the business of transportation to intrench itself as a powerful tax-gatherer and collector of tribute at these gates of commerce on this grand river, and thus absolutely control the navigation of the waters of the Columbia and its tributaries from their source to the sea, and dictate the terms of its commerce....That the waters of any one river on God's green earth, much less one so grandly magnificent in volume, length, and every other respect as the Columbia, endowed with all those elements of greatness and grandeur and moral and physical power that constitute and characterize the greatest of the great internal water-ways of the world, should be dominated and controlled by any one man or any set of men, or corporation, or company, is a standing reproach to the people or nation that tolerates or permits it. . . ."

Despite all these difficulties, the wheat moved in ever-increasing quantities down to the docks at Portland where it awaited shipment to Liverpool. The Oregon wheat fleet was one of the great transport phenomena of its day. In the autumn and winter months, the anchorages were crowded with long, lean, three- and four-masted wooden sailing vessels which had converged upon that port from Europe, India, the Orient, and Australia. Most were British, although a few other European and American ships also took part in this trade. Their numbers rapidly mounted after that first ship of 1868: five in 1870, eighty-one in the 1879-1880 season, and more than a hundred a few years later.

Once loaded with sacked grain, they were maneuvered down the Columbia by local pilots and sternwheel tugboats. The voyage around Cape Horn to Liverpool took from four to five months. . . .

All of the wheat of the Columbia Basin moved to Portland as "Walla Walla" wheat. There it was joined by approximately equal quantities exported from the Willamette Valley. At times, separate identity of the two was maintained; at other times, the cargoes were combined and shipped as "Oregon" wheat. In 1884, this total, amounting to 5,500,000 bushels, was but a sixth of the total Pacific Coast wheat export, as the Sacramento and San Joaquin valleys comprised one of the world's great wheat surplus regions....

The Walla Walla wheat grower was in competition not only with his countrymen of the Willamette, California, and the Central States, but also with farmers on every continent. The total American export accounted for only about 40 percent of the British market....

[The] competition was...complex....The variations in marketing seasons, due to the different latitudes and hemispheres of production and to the durations of voyages, insured an almost continuous flow of grain and made some regions more complementary than competitive. Quality was also an important variable. Despite the volume of Indian exports, most of the wheat was threshed by animals and was extremely dirty and of low quality. In addition, climatic hazards and inadequate transportation systems made both India and Russia unreliable sources.

Major competition came from those regions where wheat was produced on cheap land with mechanized farming as it was in the United States. The impending advance of railroads and pioneers into Manitoba and Assiniboia, into the Mallee and the Wimmera in Australia, and into the Argentine Pampa was to make it imperative that Columbia Basin farmers gain a more adequate transport system.

Such a system was to come. In later decades, the local railroad network was elaborated, competitive lines were built to the ocean ports, the river barriers were circumvented, steam replaced sail on the ocean voyage, the Panama Canal shortened the European route, and the market was broadened to include the Orient. Nevertheless, the listing of "Walla Walla" wheat on the Liverpool exchange in the 1880s was a remarkable and significant achievement. The development of this complex system of wagon, grain chute, river boat, portage railroad, and wooden sailing vessel, which together made up the longest market connection ever established in the history of wheat exporting, was a critically important stage in the economic history of the Columbia Basin.

The New Settlers on the Yakima Project, 1880-1910

by C. Brewster Coulter

In 1906, the United States government authorized a federal reclamation project in the Yakima Valley of the state of Washington. As a base for the project, the government purchased the property of the Washington Irrigation Company, a private enterprise which had developed the largest irrigation system in the Pacific Northwest. The core of the system, the Sunnyside Canal, was 42 miles long. Irrigable land "under the ditch" was estimated at 60,000 acres. Of this land, the company had sold 36,000 acres, together with the water to irrigate them, and still had title to 9,000 acres.

The Washington Irrigation Company was a real estate enterprise which had undertaken the task of irrigating the land as a necessary prerequisite to selling it. The company had no intention of staying on in business as a privately owned public utility. Its recognition that irrigation was a community or governmental function smoothed the way for this private irrigation enterprise to become a federal reclamation project.

But the company was undoubtedly influenced by another factor. During the years immediately preceding 1906, there had been a series of water shortages during the height of the irrigation season, that is, in late August. The first severe shortage was in 1903, the next in 1904, and the third and last in 1905. These shortages indicated strongly that the company had expanded its irrigation system, which was based on the natural flow of the Yakima River, about as far as it could. Or to put the crisis in terms of real estate, the Washington Irrigation Company could not sell any more land because it could not as-sure delivery of water. Therefore, it could contemplate selling its irrigation system to the United States government.

Elbert F. Blaine, attorney for the company, had offered the government an option on the Sunnyside Canal even before the water shortage in August 1905. It took about a year for the sale to be completed, not because the government was uncertain whether it wanted the system—it wanted it badly enough—the trouble was in the price. Among other things, the company asked for a free water right for the 9,000 acres of land that it still owned.

As soon as the federal government acquired title to the Sunnyside Canal, it began work on an integrated irrigation system for the project. This system included converting the lakes on the headwaters of the Yakima River into reservoirs and enlarging and extending the Sunnyside Canal. When the system was completed, the government would be able to provide more water for the 36,000 acres of land, deliver water to the 9,000 acres of Washington Irrigation Company land, and furnish water to about 10,000 acres of dry lands which were scattered among the other lands under the Sunnyside Canal and which the company had never owned. In addition, there were another 15,000 acres of land that would be served by an extension of the Sunnyside Canal to the Yakima River and by a siphon under the river.

The success of irrigation agriculture in the Yakima Valley depended in large part upon the settlers themselves and upon their ability to adjust to the realities of frontier environment. . . .

The settlers' first eight years in the Yakima

Valley were a crucial part of their adjustment to new conditions, for during these years they had to learn how to irrigate their land. Walter N. Granger—a self-taught "practical" engineer who constructed the canal, managed the water, and sold land for the Washington Irrigation Company—offered a kind of course in the rudiments of irrigation as a part of his selling technique. But all too often the settlers applied recommended procedures only to discover that the system did not work. The canal management charged the settlers with ignorance, and the settlers in turn accused the management of failing to provide enough water. This pattern of charge and countercharge persisted during the more than 20 years that the company—and Granger—controlled the irrigation system.

The settlers of the Sunnyside country—that is, of the land that became the Yakima Project—arrived in five waves of migration. The first wave consisted of stockmen-farmers who came during the early 1900s; they dug the Konewock Ditch, which later became the first three miles of the Sunnyside Canal. Hay ranchers moved in during the flush years of the 1890s. Then, at the turn of the century, a group of Dunkards, who called themselves the Christian Brothers, came to the region from the vicinity of New Lanark, Illinois. They located their Christian Cooperative Colony on the lower end of the canal, where the ditch was new and the land hitherto uncultivated. The next wave of migration came during the little "boomlet" that opened the twentieth century; these people filled the waste spaces around Sunnyside. The fifth wave came during the big boom that followed the United States Reclamation Service into the valley.

Each influx of people brought on a water shortage; each shortage caused a crisis; each crisis was of great intensity. At first, the crises arose about once a decade. But in the opening years of the twentieth century, they recurred so often that in a sense they were chronic. Yet, in each case the people were different, for each time the persons involved were the newest settlers. These crises were the dominant feature in the life of the new settlers.

The first crisis occurred during the depression years of the 1890s, when the canal company was bankrupt. The ranchers on the upper end of the Sunnyside Canal were irrigating so heavily that the receivers . . . decided to install measuring boxes on the laterals to restrict people to the rate of water delivery allowed by the contract. The settlers under the Konewock Ditch section of the canal protested. . . . Nothing came of the agitation because one of the receivers, Judge Allen, backed Granger.

During the late 1890s the water shortages disappeared, and the valley prospered. . . . The settlers began to make achievements in the production of hops and in the use of water, which provided Granger with many of the success stories he used in real estate promotion.

The ranchers of the Christian Cooperative Colony made the next contribution to the long history of friction between Granger and the new settlers. Within a year after they arrived in the Yakima Valley, the Christian Brothers were fighting with the manager of the Sunnyside Canal. S. J. Harrison, one of the leaders of the colony, lost 80 acres of alfalfa through what he claimed were the manager's mistakes. In anger, the Dunkards wrote back east, warning 100 additional members of their sect to move to Oregon instead of south-central Washington. Newspaper editors immediately turned against the agitators, for telling people to go elsewhere was a form of treason in a community which lived upon the basis of its dreams. . . .

The settlers on the first 20 miles of canal rallied to Granger's support. The old-timers persuaded 190 farmers under the canal to sign a testimonial to the excellence of Granger's administration. And then the storm blew over. At the end of 1899, Granger claimed that conditions in the valley had never been better. His optimism was based on bumper crops in the hop fields and orchards along the Konewock Ditch rather than on the withered alfalfa at Sunnyside. It was just as though there had never been a crisis during the summer.

For a while, the country prospered. A fourth wave of settlers moved into the valley to settle the country just south of Sunnyside. In 1901, the demand for water again approached the shortage stage. Thereafter, the problems involved in the efficient use of water wore on the peace of mind of all concerned. . . .

Gradually, as crisis succeeded crisis, Granger noted that there was a pattern to the shortages. . . . The latest arrivals, just south of Sunnyside, and the next to the last group, the people immediately around Sunnyside, were using far more water than the contract allowed. . . .

The promoters of the Sunnyside Canal ... set the duty of water at 160 acres. This contract allowance had no relevancy to the consumption of water on new lands. It set the duty too high. Granger finally decided that new lands required more water, so he permitted the settlers to use all the water they needed to grow a crop. He hoped that the initial flood would be confined to the first two years of irrigation and that the consumption would then drop, but it did not. In fact, five or six years passed before there was any noticeable decline in the amount of water used.

. . . Old-timers believed that every drop of water that a man diverted from a lateral into a furrow leading across a field could be absorbed by the soil by the time the water reached the last plant at the end of the furrow. Thus, there would be no waste. . . . [But] in practice the rancher found that he could not get water from a lateral into a furrow unless there was a high head of water in the lateral. Then he discovered that he had to have a clear stream running through the furrow. If the water moved so slowly that a film of dust, known as "slickens," formed on the surface, the moisture did not penetrate the soil. The settlers thus had to use much more water than the experts specified. The irrigation promoters insisted that the ranchers were wasting the very commodity that should have been most carefully preserved, for ditches and furrows of clear running water meant great quantities wasting out of the lower end. People did not yet know that this was necessary wastage.

The Sunnyside settlers discovered something else. A wind, coming before the water could seep between the furrows, would blow away any part of the soil that was not wet, leaving the wet bottom of the furrow standing like a ridge above the surface of the ground. Roscoe Sheller, one of the old-timers at Sunnyside, recalled that the only way his parents could prevent the wind from blowing the seed out of the ground was by keeping the field wet day and night until the seed sprouted—indeed, until the alfalfa covered the ground. As Sheller remembered the ordeal of that first year of irrigation, the reseeding process had to be repeated as many as six times before his father could get a "stand." Sheller felt that this repeated planting would have been bad enough with tractors and modern farm machinery, but to a horse-drawn generation it was a tragic experience, almost impossible to explain to anyone unfamiliar with its awfulness.

This Sunnyside experience helps to explain the quantities of water which the settlers had to pour on to the land in order to convert a desert into an oasis. During a period of 20 years, from 1883 to 1903, the underground water table at Sunnyside rose from 40 feet below the surface to a scant 10 feet. Most of the settlement took place during the last five years of this period. . . .

By 1903, Granger was involved in the big

shortage with the Sunnyside settlers. Something had to be done to get more water to the lower end of the canal. He tried to persuade the ranchers on the upper reaches of the canal to restrict their consumption, for it seemed obvious that they were using more water than the contract authorized. . . . Granger decided to install measuring boxes . . . on each of the sublaterals. In this way, he could measure the amount of water and, by locking the crossbar in place, restrict the quantity going to the group of hay ranchers on the sublateral.

When irrigation reached its peak that summer, men broke the weirs at night. Because each of the sublaterals supplied several ranchers, Granger found it difficult to detect the culprits and impossible to get evidence to prosecute those he could identify. Since every restrictive effort had failed, the company gave up the battle. Granger told the ranchers that, although their contracts specified a limited quantity of water, he would let them have all they needed to grow a crop. In 1904, a shortage cost the farmers under the Sunnyside Canal their third cutting of alfalfa. . . .

After the first, second, and third wages of new settlers had become old-timers, Granger evaluated them as substantial men who knew how to farm. . . . Granger considered that these people had made an important contribution to the social fabric of the Yakima Valley. . . . These people started dairies, raised beef cattle, experimented with new crops, and had new ideas. They were men of experience and vision. Wanting to operate on a large scale, some of the most successful farmers under the Sunnyside Canal had as many as 200 acres of land in alfalfa. Through them their neighbors glimpsed a new ideal of country life and of farm economy. . . .

The fifth wave of new settlers were the people with government water rights. They had come in two groups: those who had followed the Reclamation Service into the

valley and were to call themselves "book farmers"; and the homesteaders, who had arrived in Washington during the boom which followed statehood and had lived in the valley for years but had never learned how to irrigate because they had no water. As soon as Granger started to build the Sunnyside Canal, the "sagebrushers" had filed homestead claims on the alternate sections of government land which had not been a part of the railroad land grant. They tried to make a living by dryland farming, but, generally speaking, this was not possible in the Yakima Valley. . . .

And so the company built the canal. It sold land with water rights on one side of the homestead tracts and land with water rights on the other side. When the time came to irrigate, the company conducted the water past the sagebrush tracts. From an irrigation engineer's point of view, the situation was both inefficient and wasteful. . . .

Granger tried to create a solid block of irrigated land by offering to exchange a water right for one-half of a homesteader's land in return for a title deed to the other half of the land. Granger considered the offer more than fair. The company charged $30.00 for a water right to said acre. Granger proposed the sale of a water right costing $30.00 with payment in land worth $30.00, so he gained nothing by the exchange. However, the sagebrushers did not look upon the proposition in the same way. In fact, the offer only added to the already existing hostility.

One of the men to whom Granger proposed to exchange water for land was James M. Palmerston. The homesteader not only rejected the deal, but he told people that the company had refused to sell him a water right on the usual contract and had demanded payment in land. Palmerston was not the only sagebrusher to whom the offer had been made, and he was almost certainly not the only one who rejected it. From Granger's point of view, the issue had no rhyme or reason, but the sagebrushers looked upon him as an enemy. It is hard to tell how numerous the sagebrushers were among the great mass of people who bought government water rights, but, numerous or not, the sagebrushers succeeded in passing on to the new settlers with government water rights a fear of Walter N. Granger.

Some of this hostility was inevitable. In the first place, there was a continuity of irrigation management. The title to the Sunny0 side Canal was transferred from its old owners to the United States on July 26, 1906—in the middle of the irrigation season. . . . Frederick H. Newell, director of the United States Reclamation Service, asked Granger if he would go into government service as irrigation manager. This Granger was glad to do. . . .

To add to the inevitability of friction, the terms whereby the government had purchased the Sunnyside Canal required that the irrigation manager for the Reclamation Service give preference to Washington Irrigation Company lands, for the free water right for the company's lands was to be provided whenever the company wanted it. Thus, Granger could not make a clean-cut transition from his old job to his new one. In the eyes of many, he was still acting as manager for the Washington Irrigation Company.

For one reason or another, Granger came to dislike the new settlers. He defined them as poor men of all sorts and conditions—artisans, mechanics, laborers, and clerks. He believed that they had been unsuccessful in the struggle for existence back East, that they looked to the West for a last chance of acquiring a home and financial independence, but that they did not know how to farm. Although this attitude was based on dislike, it had some basis in fact. The new settlers had been clerks and mechanics, they were poor, and they were ignorant about farming. After a life of endless frustration, they were trying to make a new start on a new frontier. Granger

erred, however, in judging them to have been no good.

One of the new settlers who came to Yakima in the wake of the Reclamation Service was F. Farwell Morris. . . . As a young man, he had gone to California, where he worked in logging camps and lumber mills, but mostly on wheat ranches. He gained some knowledge of irrigation and of farming generally, but not very much. Many of the people who settled in the Yakima Valley had been through California, where they had seen what an irrigated country looked like, but they did not have much personal experience in making the system function.

In the fall of 1889, Morris moved to Washington. . . . For a while he lived in Seattle, where he probably worked in a hardware store. . . . After looking around a bit, he secured a position as a clerk in the Coffin Brothers hardware store in Yakima. When the panic of 1893 crumpled the West, the Coffins had to let some of the clerks go. Morris then moved to Boston, Massachusetts, where he married. . . .

During the years in Yakima, Morris had often talked with Henry B. Scudder, who was a Boston man, director of the First National Bank of Yakima, real estate dealer, and hop grower of some importance. Scudder had urged the younger man to go in for fruit growing. . . . When he returned to the valley in 1906, Morris . . . bought 20 acres of land just outside the town of Grandview, really just a townsite with only two houses on it, which was the next town down the canal from Sunnyside.

. . . At one of the Washington Irrigation Institute meetings, . . . [Morris] pinned the label "book farmer" upon the whole group of new settlers who had followed the Reclamation Service into the valley. Morris pointed out that "here in the irrigation valleys of the Northwest we have a big 'back to the land' movement, in some districts as many as fifty percent of the farmers are back to the landers people. Scarcely one of those has had the benefit of any training in an agricultural college. Most of them are what is [sic] called book farmers. . . ."

President Theodore Roosevelt gave additional support to the movement when he stated that the object of the government in establishing federal reclamation projects was to enable small farmers to go back on the land and to help them make a living.

The new settlers were people who had a sense of mission, who were learning the latest technical and scientific advances in agriculture out of books and learning them rapidly. . . . They found the administrative system of the reclamation unit to be unresponsive to their needs. . . . [They] thought that the lack of response went back to the fact that Walter N. Granger, the man who managed the system, hated sagebrushers and despised men who had been clerks and mechanics.

On November 18, 1908, the government posted a public notice which fixed the "estimated cost" of the Sunnyside unit of the Yakima Project at $52.00 per acre. According to the Reclamation Act, the project belonged to the water users, and the terminology suggested that the people were to have an active part in the administration of the enterprise "when the payments required by this Act are made for the major portion of the lands irrigated." As yet, the people had made no payments, but this public notice was regarded by the farmers as a sign that the enterprise had reached maturity, that the project was practically completed, and that the Sunnyside Water Users' Association was spokesman for a going concern. . . .

The question came up at the annual meeting of the water users' association on January 4, 1909. But the trustees sloughed off the issue. They had already learned that the reclamation engineers regarded any suggestion, no matter how well meant, as unwarranted criticism. . . .

When the annual meeting of the association reconvened in late January, the fight waxed hot between the new settlers and the old board of trustees. The old board represented the large landholder, real estate dealer, element in the population. The holdings of the trustees were so large that, with one vote per acre, they and a handful of friends could cast a majority of the votes. The new settlers won control of the meeting and promptly passed two new bylaws: one prohibited a person from casting more than 160-acre votes; the other prohibited voting by proxy. The meeting was adjourned again, but on February 15 the ranchers elected a new board of trustees, of which Farwell Morris, the book farmer, was a member.

This election represented a revolt of the new settlers against an old oligarchy of large landowners, who thought of the project in terms of selling the land, not of farming it. ... The election of the new board of trustees released a flood of grievances, which raised the question of why some settlers were stranded without water. . . . The issue went back to the desire of the Reclamation Service to handle water scientifically. Since Granger recognized that new lands required more water and that there was not enough of the precious fluid to supply the initial demands of all new lands at once, he recommended that additional deliveries be restricted to a specific tract of land. . . .

When the stranded settlers learned that they could not obtain water, they went to see Granger. He told them that there was nothing he could do, that he had not issued the directive which prevented him from furnishing them water. It should be noted that, while Granger was denying water to these four men on the basis of orders from headquarters, he was supplying it to some equally new arrivals who had purchased their lands from the Washington Irrigation Company. The terms by which the private company had sold out to the government had provided that it could get water from the 9,000 acres of land it still owned any time it wanted it. Thus, scientific management worked only part of the time and in restricted places.

... In petitions drawn up at a mass meeting, the settlers charged that Granger had shown repeated partiality in the distribution of water and repeated disregard for the equal rights of all water users. Thereupon, the board of trustees resolved that the removal of Granger was an imperative necessity for the best interests of both the Reclamation Service and the water users.

In the spring of 1909, Frederick H. Newell visited the Yakima Project.... The trustees of the water users' association were having a board meeting at which they were discussing several of the affidavits against Granger. Newell walked in on this meeting, but Granger stayed outside. He was not going to put himself in any position where he would have to recognize the water users' association as representing the people.

Farwell Morris... remembered that when Newell entered the room, one of the trustees, J. H. Donahue... mentioned the affidavits. Newell, in an automatic defense of Granger, retorted sharply that if the trustees had a stack of affidavits so high (holding his hands about a foot apart), it would not make any difference with the Reclamation Service. Donahue then questioned whether it was inconsequential when men testified that their crops were drying up, while people alongside had plenty of water.

During the summer of 1909, Secretary of the Interior Richard A. Ballinger and the Senate Committee on the Reclamation of Arid Lands inspected the government's irrigation projects. On August 27, 1909, the Senate Committee met with the water users' association at Sunnyside. Secretary Ballinger presided, and Newell was seated at the head table. The new settlers took advantage of the opportunity to air their grievances against the administration of the Yakima Project....

Although Ballinger supported Granger openly, he gave one of the officers of the Reclamation Service "a very distinct impression" that the government should ask Granger to resign. Arthur P. Davis, chief engineer of the Reclamation Service, passed the word on. The recommendation put the Yakima Valley into turmoil. Granger's friends made a desperate effort to save him.

In an attempt to recapture control of the water users' association, a group of "substantial" landowners and businessmen organized a Unity and Progress Club to represent "the conservative people." But the conservative people simply were not numerous enough, and on the election night the new board of trustees countered the assault of the Unity and Progress Club with a cartoon entitled "Donahue Did It." This showed... Donahue holding the field, with Newell and Granger knocked down, and Ballinger climbing the fence in full retreat. The cartoon was a decisive factor in the election, for it unified the ranks of the sagebrushers and the book farmers in support of the new board. A few days later, Granger handed in his resignation.

The years after Granger's resignation were ones of relative quiet, but a few things did happen. The Reclamation Service gradually gave more attention to the wishes of those who were trying to farm the land.... Hardships continued, but gradually the people learned how to irrigate, and the underground water table rose until drainage became a major problem in the lower valley. New issues, involving horticulture on one hand and fruit marketing on the other, came to the fore. Finally, even the trustees of the Sunnyside Water Users' Association decided that they liked the Reclamation Service.

The Mystique of
Grand Coulee Dam and the Reality
of the Columbia Basin Project

by Paul C. Pitzer

The Grand Coulee Dam is one of the major tourist attractions in Washington. Every year, thousands of people travel to eastern Washington to visit the huge structure. Most have heard about the dam's extraordinary size and the power it produces, yet many do not realize that the green fields and productive farms they pass on the trip are a byproduct of the great dam. There is a significant contrast between the mystique of Grand Coulee Dam and the reality of the Columbia Basin irrigation project.

In 1933, the newly elected Roosevelt administration began to finance and construct Grand Coulee Dam and the Columbia Basin Project. The venture was controversial, especially in the East, where some disapproved of public power and others objected to expensive western reclamation efforts. A few questioned the wisdom of putting such a large and costly undertaking seemingly in the middle of nowhere, far from any market for its electricity.

To counter criticism, backers of the dam and its builder, the Bureau of Reclamation, conducted a public relations campaign that lasted over a decade. . . . "It has been estimated," wrote popular historian Stewart Holbrook, "that a definitive shelf of Grand Coulee books, pamphlets, magazine articles and newspaper stories would run to more lineal feet, or greater poundage, or would... far exceed all other writings which . . . have been devoted to . . . the Columbia and all of its tributaries from source to mouth." . . .

Freelance journalist Richard L. Neuberger underscored the success of the effort when he wrote in 1942, "Everyone in America has heard of Grand Coulee."

Neuberger, more than anyone else, helped build Grand Coulee's image. A liberal Democrat, he strongly endorsed construction of dams by the federal government, and he readily joined the ranks of Grand Coulee boosters. "Man's Greatest Structure," he called it in 1936, and a year later he labeled it "The Biggest Thing on Earth." He went on to write about it in *Harper's, The Christian Science Monitor, Nation, The New Republic,* and *Survey Graphic,* not to mention his 1938 book, *Our Promised Land.* Neuberger often repeated the claim that the United States was building the biggest man-made thing on the face of the Earth. Other publications picked up the phrase, and in its many variations it became Grand Coulee Dam's standard metaphor.

Neuberger was not the only source of Grand Coulee propaganda. An article in *Barron's* in December 1939 began, "Out on the Pacific Coast the New Deal has started a power project that ultimately will make Muscle Shoals and Boulder Dam look like adventures with building blocks." Six months later, *Newsweek* called Grand Coulee the "greatest power, reclamation, and flood control project ever conceived," although the accompanying map placed Grand Coulee near Wenatchee, indicating that some in the East were a little hazy about the location of the great dam. *Newsweek* had also overlooked Robert Bradford Marshall's 1919 plan for a California water development project, which was ten times larger than the Columbia Basin Project.

The *Seattle Times,* among others, called Grand Coulee "The Eighth Wonder of the World." That inflated sobriquet caught on and became part of the dam's legend even before the first bucket of concrete was poured. "The World's Greatest Dam" will create an electrified paradise, promised *Popular Science Monthly* in 1936. It compared the dam to five of the great pyramids of Egypt.

In 1935, while Congress debated authorization and funding for Grand Coulee, Rufus Woods put out a special eight-page edition of his *Wenatchee Daily World.* Its headline declared that reclamation engineers at Grand Coulee Dam were harnessing "Two Million Wild Horses!" Woods sent copies to every legislator in Washington, D.C. It would be wrong, he wrote, for the country not to complete "the World's Greatest Project.". . .

No one doubted that Grand Coulee Dam was big. But as early as 1933, when Representative Knute Hill claimed that the dam would be the largest of man's structures, the *Oregonian* suggested that the congressman had overlooked the Great Wall of China. The reality, as historian Murray Morgan correctly wrote, is that Grand Coulee Dam was "the largest concrete structure in the world, one of the biggest things built since the Great Wall of China." But the backers of Grand Coulee were successful in making it seem to be the biggest, and their influence was worldwide. In 1939, the *China Weekly Review* reprinted an article written in Shanghai which said, "From the standpoint of general interest, the Grand Coulee Dam is the largest monument ever made by man on this earth.". . .

In 1938, Neuberger called the dam the "World's Greatest Engineering Wonder." Indeed, the engineering and construction accomplishments at Grand Coulee were formidable. . . . In 1955, . . . the American Society of Civil Engineers listed Grand Coulee Dam and the Columbia Basin Project as one of the seven civil engineering wonders of the United States. However, as D. C. Riddle, chief engineer for one of the two conglomerates that built the dam, wrote for *Civil Engineering* in 1936, "In working out the construction problems presented on such a vast scale at Grand Coulee Dam, no startling novelties have been attempted. On the contrary, the selection of tools and methods was based on proven experience." An editorial a year later in *Pacific Builder and Engineer* added, "Reclamation engineers are fond of saying that `Boulder [Dam] was just a laboratory we built in order to find out how to build Coulee.'"

. . . The mystique created in the 1930s [has been] perpetuated. In a 1983 article, the *Wenatchee World* stated, "Grand Coulee Dam stands as one of the paramount construction projects of the 20th Century. . . . It was a task that tested to the limit man's knowledge of engineering in the 1930s."

Commenting in 1934 on one of the problems relating to construction of Grand Coulee, an article in *Public Utilities Fortnightly* stated that the anticipated surplus of Grand Coulee power would be utilized only if some miracle happened: "There might be a war which would crowd the Pacific Northwest with eager workers and their Saturday nights with wassail.". . .

In October 1940, the government declared the dam a national defense project. A few days later, a sizable quantity of electricity from the as yet unfinished generators was sold, in advance, by the Bonneville Power Administration to the Aluminum Company of America. [The power] was earmarked for defense purposes. Interior Secretary Harold L. Ickes urged faster completion of the Grand Coulee generators. Work on the second and third generators was speeded up, while the fourth through sixth were granted high priority by the War Production Board. The Bureau of Reclamation and the press throughout the Northwest and the nation heralded each new generator and boasted of the enormous contribution made to the war effort by every increase in power output.

In February 1944, the sixth large Grand Coulee unit turned for the first time. But after the sixth, no more of the anticipated 18 generators were installed during the war. On October 27, 1942, the War Production Board had suspended the priority for Grand Coulee Dam and stopped work on the second powerhouse entirely. The decisive battles of the war were over before the last two generators began production, and even earlier it was clear that further capacity at Grand Coulee would have no effect on the outcome of the fighting. In all, about one-third of the planes built in the United States during World War II used aluminum produced from power generated at Grand Coulee Dam.

Grand Coulee power went not only to aluminum production, but also to what was then a "mystery project" at Hanford. As the *Wenatchee Daily World* reflected in 1948, "It was this hydroelectric power which made possible the development of the atomic bomb at Hanford—development which shortened the war and saved the lives of thousands of American boys and billions of dollars." . . . Promoters of the dam . . . credited Grand Coulee directly with the victory. But it stretches the point to write about Grand Coulee, as journalist Marc Reisner did in 1986, that "it probably won the Second World War."

While Coulee may not have won the war, the war clearly won Grand Coulee. The sudden need for large blocks of power ended claims by detractors such as Republican Representative Francis D. Culkin of New York, that nobody would ever buy the electricity and that it would have to be sold to "Jack Robinson Rabbit." If nothing else, World War II made Grand Coulee Dam an unquestioned economic success. It was this sudden and overwhelming success that solidified

the mystique of Grand Coulee Dam. . . .

The human cost of Grand Coulee has also been exaggerated. Craig Sprankle, Information Officer for the Bureau of Reclamation at Grand Coulee Dam, notes that tourists continue to ask if any workmen were entombed in the dam when it was built. Grand Coulee publicity in the 1930s frequently centered on the speed at which contractors poured the concrete. Nearly 80 men did die during construction, but no one was buried in the process. What Joseph Stevens wrote about Hoover Dam could be equally true of Grand Coulee: "The idea of workers forever entombed in the great structure they had helped build was so irresistibly poetic, so deliciously macabre, that it became the basis for the most enduring legend of Hoover Dam. . . ."

Grand Coulee Dam was, then, the biggest masonry dam ever constructed, but it was not the biggest manmade thing on Earth. It was a notable engineering accomplishment, but it was not the greatest engineering wonder as was claimed by its champions. . . . The power it generated facilitated the Allied victory in World War II, but Grand Coulee hardly did the job single-handedly. And finally, there are no bodies buried in the concrete. . . . Indisputable, however, is the bigger-than-life mystique created by Grand Coulee Dam advocates which persists today.

That pervasive mystique masks the reality that Grand Coulee Dam is but one element of the larger Columbia Basin Project. For at Grand Coulee, reclamation and power generation are inextricably linked. The huge dam creates a lake from which irrigation water is drawn. Power from the generators turns the pumps that raise the water about 270 feet into an equalizing reservoir. The sale of the rest of the electricity pays all the costs of power generation and subsidizes most of the reclamation bill. . . .

The symbiotic relationship between power and irrigation was the vision of newspaper editor Rufus Woods: of lawyer Billy Clapp, who is credited with first suggesting construction of the dam in 1918: and of James O'Sullivan, another lawyer. They were typical of the professionals and businessmen in eastern Washington who saw irrigation of the one-million-acre-plus project as a way to build an agricultural-industrial empire in the Columbia Basin. That empire would provide farms with cheap, abundant water, and farmers, in turn, would provide a market for a growing industrial complex.

In the 1930s, the New Deal added the aspect of planning to the vision. New Deal historian Richard Lowitt called it the goal of the "Planned Promised Land." The idea was to create small irrigated farms and self-sufficient communities where the economy was controlled, soil fertility assured, and productivity guaranteed. The rich reclaimed land would replace submarginal land in other locations. The project would benefit perhaps 80,000 families, including many dust bowl refugees.

In 1937, the Columbia River Basin Anti-Speculation Act formalized the goals by limiting irrigated farms to 40 and 80 acres. Owners of larger tracts would be required to sell their excess land. Under the new law, landowners formed three irrigation districts and signed contracts with the government for delivery of water.

. . . The Columbia Basin Joint Investigations, a series of 28 studies involving over 40 government and private agencies, . . . recommended . . . [some changes, and in 1943] the Columbia Basin Project Act . . . allowed the size of farms on the project to range from 10 to 160 acres, depending on the quality of the land.

World War II delayed reclamation construction for about ten years. Finally, in 1952, the first water from behind Grand Coulee Dam arrived on the land. But with the water, unforeseen problems developed. Unwilling to accept the land limitations, many wheat farmers, mostly on the east side of the project, withdrew over 300,000 acres. Post-war inflation raised construction costs beyond anything anticipated. And drainage of surplus irrigation water quickly became an unexpected headache. Only $8 million had been allocated to pay for drainage facilities, and many times that amount was needed. Furthermore, farmers--caught between higher costs, the need to mechanize, and declining farm prices—chafed under the landowership limitations.

The Bureau of Reclamation attempted to negotiate a new contract with higher repayments in order to cover the rising costs. But the farmers argued that power revenues should pay the bills, as had been promised in the past. The bitter controversy continued from 1954 until 1962, when both sides finally agreed on revised repayment contracts. They raised the average cost of water delivery for each acre of land from $85 to $163.50. The repayment period, however, was extended from 40 to 50 years, so that the cost per year was actually reduced in the initial years of the contract.

In 1957, after intense lobbying by project supporters, Congress amended the anti-speculation limitations of the Columbia Basin Project Act. Despite objections from the Bureau of Reclamation, the new law allowed any individual to own up to 160 acres, while a husband and wife might own 320 acres. The law also liberalized leasing restrictions and allowed farmers to rent land and receive water as long as they did not own property in excess of the limits.

Although resolution of these problems provided increased money for drainage work and lessened tensions between farmers and the Bureau of Reclamation, the episode had repercussions. After 1960, and especially after 1965, enlargement of the project slowed appreciably. Only about 40,000 acres have been added since 1968. Today, just over 550,000 acres, about half of the contemplated project, are under the ditch.

On October 12, 1982, President Ronald Reagan signed the Reclamation Reform Act, . . . updating the Reclamation (or Newlands) Act of 1902. The new law raised landowership limits on all government irrigation projects to 960 acres and allowed farmers to pay the full cost of water delivery on anything over the 960-acre limit. It was a far distance from the New Deal vision of self-sufficient farms of 40 and 80 acres planned almost 50 years earlier. In 1973, there were 2,290 farms operating on the Columbia Basin Project, an average of 240 acres each, supporting something fewer than the 80,000 families predicted by earlier visionaries. Twenty-four farms exceed 900 acres, and four are 2,000 acres or larger. This does not account for farmers who may be renting additional project land and may actually be operating larger tracts.

Changing conditions, changing economics, and the understandable desire of farmers to live better than on a self-sufficient subsistence level altered the visions for the planned promised land. Transmission lines carried the power away from the Columbia Basin, and that, combined with shipping costs to distant markets, prevented realization of the agricultural-industrial empire that Rufus Woods had anticipated. . . .

Yet, since the middle 1960s, a new organization, composed largely of professionals and businessmen, has lobbied the government to complete the Columbia Basin Project. The Columbia Basin Development League argues, as did its predecessors, that increased irrigation will enrich eastern Washington and benefit the state and the Pacific Northwest.

But there are unanswered questions. Who will pay the cost of such a construction, now estimated at well over $2 billion? Is there enough water both to generate needed power and to irrigate more land? Is more reclaimed land really needed? Will farmers on new irrigated land pay more or the same as farmers in older, adjacent areas? How much should power ratepayers subsidize irrigation?

In 1992, the completed Grand Coulee will be 50 years old. The mystique of the giant dam continues undiminished. But in the shadow of that mystique, the reclamation issue continues to raise questions. . . . The vision of the agricultural-industrial empire of north-central Washington and the New Deal's goal of the "Planned Promised Land" for that region have not materialized.

On the positive side, the project has not generated a huge self-perpetuating bureaucracy, and it is doubtful that the Bureau of Reclamation is a "power to reckon with," as Donald Worster found that it was in California. But the Bureau does have politically powerful advocates who persistently push for the project's completion. The next few years may determine whether or not that will happen.

The Coon-Neuberger Debates of 1955
"Ten Dam Nights in Oregon"
by Bert E. Swanson and Deborah Rosenfeld

. . . In 1955, Congressman Sam Coon and Senator Richard L. Neuberger used the debate . . . to educate their fellow Oregonians on the complex issue of developing hydroelectric power and distributing the benefits equitably—and, not incidentally, to gain advantage in the Oregon political arena. . . .

One of the primary problems facing the residents of Oregon and other states in the Pacific Northwest is that of transforming the region's economic status from a colonial dependence on extractive raw materials to one of diversified and expanded industry. The region suffers because of its great distance from suitable markets for its products and the resulting dependence upon costly transportation. In addition, the region lacks a balanced energy base, which is a fundamental prerequisite to industrial expansion. It has modest coal reserves, but neither petroleum nor natural gas reserves has as yet been discovered. Its sole energy resource is hydroelectric power, and this is available in great abundance.

Since the end of World War II, the situation has assumed even more serious proportions. By 1955, the battle over the development of the area's single major source of energy had reached a virtual impasse—and a severe power shortage was being predicted. Already the shortage had, in effect, curtailed expansion of the aluminum industry, which depends almost entirely upon uninterruptible "dump" power. This was a matter of great concern to the entire region, for it was convinced that low-cost hydroelectric power was essential to its plans for attracting the new industries necessary to diversity its economic base. The Pacific Northwest was faced with—and still faces—the direct and critical problem of developing fully its one major energy resource. As Senator Richard L. Neuberger argued before the Portland City Club [on April 26, 1957]:

If you and I are marooned on a desert island where only oranges grow, do you spend all your time telling me how much more nutritious would be eggs or beefsteak or Irish potatoes? No, you join with me in exploiting and developing our orange crop to the maximum. Why should we in the Northwest listen to people who scoff at our federal power system by telling us that transportation or local markets are a better way of luring new payrolls? We don't have the other advantages, we did have the power advantage.

The major public policy problem of the region is to determine who shall continue to develop its hydroelectric potential. Shall it be the federal government, under conditions advocated by the New Deal of Franklin D. Roosevelt and Harry Truman? Shall it be the private utilities? Shall it be a partnership of the two, as proposed by the Eisenhower administration?

In 1950, Congress authorized the United States Army Corps of Engineers to construct the John Day Dam. . . . The damsite lies 95 miles east of Portland, just below the mouth of the John Day River. The structure will house 13 85,000-KW generators which will produce 5.2 billion KWH of prime energy annually. The reservoir behind the dam will provide 595,000 acre-feet of flood-control storage with irrigation benefits. The plans include two fish ladders and one navigation lock. Compared with other dam facilities on the Columbia River, John Day is considered a medium-sized project.

Except for the usual adverse comments expressed by the commercial fishing interests, the Yakima Indians (who would lose their traditional fishing rights), and those opposing the land inundation features, the construction of the John Day Dam . . . received little opposition during public hearings in the spring of 1953. In fact, this "noncontroversial" project appeared to be scheduled for an early start as a compromise move in the bitter struggle over the high Hell's Canyon Dam. By the fall of 1953, the height of the John Day Dam came under attack from the Portland Chamber of Commerce, which called for a 250-foot reservoir level rather than the 292-foot level planned by the army engineers.

On March 10, 1954, Secretary of the Interior Douglas McKay, former governor of Oregon, met with Thomas W. Delzell, chairman of the board of the Portland General Electric Company, to discuss the proposed John Day Dam. McKay denied that the project was "being seriously considered" as a partnership plan. A company spokesman maintained that "no special consideration has been given by any group of private or public utilities for assuming the John Day project." The Portland *Oregonian*, however, sensing new developments, issued a note of caution the next day: "Our enthusiasm is restrained over the possibilities that utility companies may seek to build the John Day Dam on the Columbia . . . we would prefer to see these big multi-purpose dams built by a regional nonprofit corporation—if the federal government is calling a half."

Two Oregon political leaders involved in the John Day development differed in their reactions to the partnership proposal. Secretary McKay thought that the proposal indicated that the administration's "partnership suggestion is being accepted in the Northwest." Senator Guy Cordon, Republican chairman of the Senate Interior Committee, who was about to engage in a vigorous re-election campaign against State Senator Richard Neuberger, called the proposal intriguing, but emphasized that he would prefer to see "all the hydroelectric systems in the Pacific Northwest publicly owned. . . ." The *Oregon Journal* [on March 10, 1954] editorially termed the proposal the "most imaginative 'power partnership' offer so far made to Uncle Sam."

Within two months Senator Cordon and Congressman Sam Coon, Republicans from eastern Oregon where the project was located, introduced partnership bills (S. 3510 and H.R. 9306). Under their proposal, private utilities would put up $164 million, slightly more than half of the total cost of the dam, estimated at $320 million. Reaction to the Cordon-Coon partnership proposal was mixed. State Senator Neuberger, now an active candidate for the United States Senate against Cordon, called the plan disastrous. Senator Wayne Morse, who by now had switched his party loyalty to the Democrats, continued to move for federal planning money, saying that "the dam must be planned before it is built, under either arrangement." The Oregon Rural Electric Cooperative Association passed a resolution opposing the Cordon-Coon bill.

Neuberger's narrow victory over Cordon in the 1954 election left only Coon to continue advocating a partnership John Day project in Congress. Coon's new bill (H.R. 5789) stipulated that the utilities were willing to underwrite $273 million or 88 percent of the cost. Neuberger immediately pointed out: "It is evident that the power assets of the John Day site are so valuable that the private utilities are willing to up their bid at least $100,000,000." Coon in turn characterized Neuberger's statement as "typical of the reactionary, obstructionist tactics used by those who hope to prevent prompt development of the hydroelectric resources of the Pacific Northwest." With this exchange, the battle was begun.

Congressman Sam Coon was a 52-year-old cattle rancher from eastern Oregon. An easygoing, friendly man, he proclaimed that 20 years on the range with his horse and dog hardly prepared him for debate with the senator from the big city. But Coon was not as unlearned as he led his audiences to believe. He had a degree in business administration from the University of Idaho. He had served a term in the Oregon State Senate before being elected to Congress in the Eisenhower boom of 1952.

Sam Coon . . . represented the people of eastern Oregon and he knew the area well, but he had no real passion for political party affairs and only a slight grasp of the problems involved in developing the hydroelectric resources of the Pacific Northwest.

Senator Richard L. Neuberger, Democrat from Portland, was a prolific writer on the politics and history of the Pacific Northwest. He was ten years younger than Coon, but his graying hair and sallow complexion made him appear much older. Although he was from the big city, he convinced his rural audiences of his sincerity. A merciless opponent, he seldom let a point pass without turning it over and over, with the result that neither Coon nor the audience was able to forget the significance of the issue being debated. . . . He successfully ran for a seat in the Oregon State Senate, where he served for five years as a member of a small but vocal Democratic minority. In 1954, he dramati-

cally defeated incumbent Guy Cordon for the United States Senate, by a narrow margin of 2,500 votes.

Neuberger . . . was well grounded in the regional problems of resource development, having been a press official for the Bonneville Power Administration. His interest in and concern for the resources of his beloved Pacific Northwest soon earned him the reputation in the United States Senate as "Mr. Conservation." Politics was his constant preoccupation. He responded to its challenge and felt that everyone else should do so too.

On May 4, 1955, Senator Neuberger wrote to Representative Coon challenging him to debate the merits of the John Day Dam partnership bill. . . .

By the end of June, two months after the challenge had been issued, Coon and Neuberger had reached a tentative agreement of the rules of debate and the schedule of their appearances in the ten largest cities within the Second Congressional District. The cities selected were Baker, Bend, Burns, Hood River, Klamath Falls, La Grande, Lakeview, The Dalles, Ontario, and Pendleton. Their populations ranged from 3,200 to 19,500. The local sponsors were to be such service clubs as the Chambers of Commerce, Toastmasters, and the Young Democrat and Young Republican clubs. The debates were to be held in school auditoriums; the moderators were to be ministers, Junior Chamber of Commerce members, school officials, a judge, an attorney, and a realtor. . . .

Neuberger's phrasing of the question was accepted by Coon: "Agreed, the John Day Dam is in the public interest." As proposed in H.R. 5789, the John Day Dam was to be a multi-purpose project designed to provide 1,105,000 kilowatts of hydroelectric power, slack-water navigation of the Columbia River from Bonneville Dam to Pasco, Washington, flood control, and irrigation potential. The total cost of the project was estimated at $310 million; it was to be financed by a "partnership" arrangement whereby the local private and public utilities would furnish $273 million or 88 percent of the cost as prepayment for the power component, and the remaining nonreimbursable facilities would be financed by the federal government. The federal government would design, construct, operate, maintain, and own the dam, but the local partners would pay for its operation, maintenance, and replacement of power and related parts. The project would be operated according to the comprehensive plan for the Columbia River and would be integrated into the Northwest Power Pool. The terms of the partnership would run for a 50-year period.

Congressman Coon's affirmative argumentation was a defense of the partnership principle and of the John Day proposal in particular. He contended that the rapidly expanding power needs of the region could not be met by the federal program alone and that the impending power shortage would produce a "brownout" similar to the one experienced in the region at the conclusion of the war. The power needs of the area required the construction of the equivalent of one Bonneville Dam a year or $1 million a day for the next ten years. At the current rate of federal appropriations, he estimated that this would take 27 years.

Coon pointed out that the Pacific Northwest, which had only 4 percent of the nation's population, had received 33-1/3 percent of the nation's public works appropriations. (Richard L. Neuberger's rebuttal: No other section of the country complains when it receives a disproportionate share of public expenditure. Where else would you spend this money to harness rivers than where the rivers are located by nature?)

Coon insisted that this ratio was bound to

be reduced because congressmen from other sections of the country had begun to press for greater appropriations to provide relief and safeguards against floods which their regions had recently experienced. As he saw it, three methods were available to meet the impending power crisis: "We can raise taxes, we can increase deficit spending which will raise the national debt, or we can use money provided by local interests, as projected in my John Day Dam proposal." The partnership proposal would mean more power sooner, more industrial development, and more employment. (RLN rebuttal: The region underwent its greatest growth after the development of the federal power program and low-cost power.) . . .

Coon stated that the two areas in the country with power shortages were the Tennessee Valley and the Pacific Northwest, in both of which the federal government was the major developer. (RLN rebuttal: This was true because these were the two areas in the country with the cheapest power costs. Both the Tennessee Valley Authority and the Bonneville Power Authority had encouraged high levels of usage through low cost. This shortage could be ended by doubling the cost, but that was not the answer to the problem.)

Coon noted that the partnership concept was not new, that it had first been used by Theodore Roosevelt in 1908. Since then there had been three such projects under Taft, six under Wilson, six under Coolidge, two under Hoover, six under Franklin D. Roosevelt, and two under Truman. Coon concluded by striking out at "reactionary thinkers who cannot progress with the times. We need new methods to meet our power needs."

Senator Neuberger prepared an extensive outline statement with 35 points in opposition to the John Day partnership proposal. He viewed the "falling water" of the Columbia River as the greatest asset of the Pacific Northwest. "It provides our only natural resource of energy to expand industry—to work for us in our homes, farms, and factories." But these benefits could be obtained "only if the river is developed to its fullest, at the lowest possible costs."

Senator Neuberger believed that "partnership power" would be high-cost power. It would set up a two-price system: (1) the public power already being distributed throughout the region at a uniform "postage stamp" rate based on the low-cost kilowatts from such dams as the Grand Coulee and Bonneville, which had better sites than the John Day Dam and which had been built when prices were low: and (2) the power financed by the private utilities paying higher rates of interest on money borrowed, which would mean a 13 percent increase in the cost of power for each increase of one percent in the interest rate. Concentrating on the economics of partnership, Neuberger envisioned the "partners" paying the government $273 million over a period of 50 years for power they could sell at retail for approximately $5 billion!

Neuberger turned his attack on the private power lobby and Secretary of the Interior Douglas McKay. He pointed out that partnership interests had in the 1930s predicted that Bonneville and Grand Coulee dams would be "white elephants" without a market for their power production. These same interests issued a detailed report in 1946 urging no more federal dams because the Northwest would have a surplus of 780,000 kilowatts by 1955. Neuberger characterized such a policy as "deliberately encouraging a vacuum, in which a surrender to so-called 'partnership' would seem to be the only possible alternative."

Referring to the McKay policy of spending $1.8 billion on the Upper Colorado project,

Neuberger asked: "Does our Secretary of Interior think the public should be saddled with mediocre power sites, while utility monopolies take over the first-class sites like Hells Canyon and John Day?" (Coon's rebuttal: The Senator must have been a little befuddled—the topic was the John Day Dam, not the Colorado River. As for Hell's Canyon, why had three Democratic Congresses failed to pass a Hell's Canyon bill?)

Neuberger quoted Palmer Hoyt, editor of the Denver *Post*, a former editor of the *Oregonian*, and lifelong Republican, who called for McKay's resignation: "The people of the United States need a Secretary of the Interior who will act boldly in the demonstrated public interest . . . one who will not retreat behind the fatuous doubletalk about 'socialism,' the pre-eminence of local interests or that frightfully abused phrase 'free private enterprise' which is touchingly symbolized by what the late Mr. Ickes aptly described as the 'barefoot boys of Wall Street.'"

Neuberger concluded his prepared statement by asking, "Do you think Bonneville, Grand Coulee and McNary Dams have been good for Oregon and the Northwest? Would you do away with these projects? Do you think any one of them ever would have been built if the McKay 'partnership' policy had been in effect back in 1933?"

The ten nights of debate produced several additional major points and counterpoints.

STATEMENT (Coon): "The Senator would rather see Oregon become a desert than have power produced by either public or private agencies.

REPLY (Neuberger): The John Day bill does not "play fair with future generations. The people should look ahead to the future and consider any moves today in light of how they will affect others 50 years from now."

STATEMENT (Coon): The farmers of Oregon all had electricity because private enterprise brought it to the rural areas of America.

REPLY (Neuberger): "It is ridiculous for Congressman Coon to claim these private companies are concerned about rural users. Until the Bonneville system and the REA [Rural Electrification Administration] came into creation, the private companies had brought energy to only 21 percent of Oregon farms. Federal competition brought energy to 98 percent of Oregon's rural residents."

REBUTTAL (Coon): "It looks to me in these debates like Senator Neuberger may be thinking deeper than he's talking. He says a few friendly words—even though very few—for private enterprise in the electric power field. But I think he's trying to force Oregon into public power when he insists on the preference clause as it is."

STATEMENT (Coon): The socializers and federalizers had cast doubt on private enterprise. "I want you to know I am for private enterprise from the peanut vendor on the corner to large industry. Private enterprise is what made this country great."

REPLY (Neuberger): "It has been implied that I am against private enterprise. That is not true. I believe in private enterprise. I believe in bringing to the Northwest industries that will provide many jobs and the only way to bring it is to have low-cost government power." The private utilities were not discriminated against. "In the last 16 years Bonneville has sold 28 million kilowatt hours of current to public organizations and public concerns. Private utilities pay Bonneville the rate of 2.34 mills per kilowatt hour, while public bodies pay 2.81 mills."

STATEMENT (Neuberger): "I think the public has a right to know who drafted legislation which would dispose of our Columbia River power resources." Neuberger read a letter concerning a draft of the bill written by Kinsey M. Robinson, president of Washington Water Power Company.

REPLY (Coon): Coon pointed out that he had consulted with a number of people in drafting the bill. "Maybe the Senator doesn't prepare legislation that way. I doubt if he had any help in preparing the bill that wouldn't let you powder your face to appear on television." Robinson stated that Neuberger was "talking through his hat."

STATEMENT (Neuberger): Congressman Coon should stand shoulder to shoulder with Senator Wayne Morse and Neuberger to fight for the needed appropriation on the Columbia River.

REPLY (Coon): "That might take a lot of moving around. One time Senator Morse was against Democrats and now he is for them. He was for President Eisenhower and now he's against him. I don't know what he will be next year."

STATEMENT (Neuberger): "The debate has ended here and now." (This was his response to an admission by Coon that private power would be more costly than BPA power, a contention that Neuberger had been making night after night.)

REPLY (Coon): "All Bonneville power is sold at wholesale rates. Comparing retail rates with Bonneville wholesale rates is like comparing timber in the forest with 2 x 4's in a lumber yard."

REBUTTAL (Neuberger): Partnership meant higher rates for power which would "choke off Oregon's chances for new payrolls. Farmers in Oregon must ship their surplus produce 1,000 miles east at high freight costs and this has retarded agriculture in Oregon. Our one hope for a consumer market close to home is low-cost power, making possible big industry which relies on electricity for fuel."

Senator Neuberger and Congressman Coon were not the only participants in the debates. Their capacity audiences responded directly and meaningfully in the question-and-answer periods at the conclusion of each debate. They were concerned not only with the construction of the dam. They sought information on the financing, operation, and maintenance of the facility. They wanted to know who would own and operate the dam, who would pay taxes on the partnership project, and whether tax rates would go up if the facility were built and operated solely by the federal government. They asked about rate structure, whether industry would continue to receive the low BPA industrial rate, and whether existing irrigation subsidies would be adversely affected. Some questions related to regional economic development in terms of industrial diversification and the use of electric energy to minimize dependence on timber and agriculture.

The audiences openly expressed ideological concern. Many of the listeners believed that the federal power program in the Pacific Northwest was verging on socialism because the federal government had developed half of the energy resources of the region. They repeatedly asked Senator Neuberger, "Where do you draw the line on socialization—are timber, mining, oil and gas production and farming next?"

There was much speculation as to the probable outcome of the debates with regard to the issue, the debaters, and the audiences. Nearly everyone was cautious about predicting the effect on the John Day proposal itself, for it was obvious that the debates would materially affect congressional action on the bill. In addition, there was a feeling that the debates would have some national importance in clarifying the federal power policy shift from the New Deal program to the partnership program advocated by the Eisenhower-McKay administration. . . .

. . . Coon lost the election, and the Republicans lost a seat in Congress. The John Day partnership proposal was defeated in Congress, and the dam is now nearing completion as an all-federal project. Coon was given a compensatory position in Peru by the Eisenhower Administration. . . .

Longview
The Career of a Washington Model City
by Carl Abbott

"The growth of Longview has been like the painting of a beautiful picture. Nature prepared the canvas—a vast plain lying at the confluence of two rivers and rimmed round with fir-clad hills. The patron at whose command the painting was made was R. A. Long, founder and chairman of the board of the Long-Bell Lumber Company. The painters were the city planners and the men . . . in charge of the development of the city. The brushes of men, money, and materials are at work; the canvas begins to gleam with color. The plan begins to take shape."

When B. L. Lambuth offered this colorful invocation of Longview in 1926, the "model city" was four years old and thriving. It had already attracted substantial attention among planners and engineers with articles in professional periodicals such as *American City, Parks and Recreation, Proceedings of the American Society of Civil Engineers,* and *Architect and Engineer,* as well as British and Canadian planning journals. The public was simultaneously being introduced to Longview through an advertising campaign in the *Literary Digest, Saturday Evening Post,* and regional periodicals. A typical full-page spread proclaimed the remarkable location, climate, and opportunities in the new industrial city of the Pacific Northwest. It was beautiful, permanent, clean, moral, growing, thriving. It offered "genuine opportunity to persons who seek a place for industry, who seek property investment, who seek an ideal place in which to live."

In conception and location, Longview was a byproduct of the changing regional struc-ture of the wood products industry. The Long-Bell Lumber Company of Kansas City had grown by cutting and marketing south-ern pine lumber. By the end of World War I, it was clear that good timber was growing scarce in the South but was still abundant in old-growth stands in the Pacific Northwest. In 1918 and 1919, Long-Bell responded by purchasing tens of thousands of acres of forest land in northern California, southern Oregon, and especially in southwestern Washington, where the company bought 70,000 acres in Lewis and Cowlitz counties from the Weyerhaeuser Timber Company. Wesley Vandercook, the company's chief engineer, studied Astoria, Portland, and the confluence of the Cowlitz and Columbia riv-ers as sites for a mill and shipping facilities. Early in 1921, the company acquired the Cowlitz site. Its advantages included rail access, proximity to the timber stands, and deep water for overseas shipments.

Working backwards, company chairman R. A. Long realized that a successful mill operation employing several thousand work-ers would generate and require a substantial town. Early in 1922, he purchased not only the mill site but also the rest of the valley, a total of 14,000 acres. His decision was to develop his own "industrial city" to house his workers and to take advantage of ex-pected regional growth with the expansion of lumbering and related businesses on the lower Columbia. In one sense, his intention was preemptive and protective, to prevent haphazard and undesirable development near his mill. At the same time, the erection of a new city offered Long the chance to fulfill what he clearly saw as a personal duty to match business success with civic accomplishment.

For specific plans, Long drew on an informal "Kansas City school" of urban planning that had developed in the prairie metropolis. The dominant figure was Jesse C. Nichols, a highly successful real estate developer who had made his Country Club district of Kansas City a national showcase for good urban design. As a friend of R. A. Long, Nichols visited the Cowlitz River site in 1922 and offered basic advice on planning layout and regulation. Also involved was George Kessler, the designer of Kansas City's nationally known park system and consultant to dozens of other cities.

The third important figure was S. Herbert Hare, a young city planner who had done substantial work for Nichols on the Country Club district. Whereas Kessler provided a connection to the great landscape architecture tradition of nineteenth century America, Hare represented a new group of professional planning consultants, such as John Nolen, Charles Cheney, and Harland Bartholomew, whose interest was the planning of efficient and economical cities. In the spring of 1922, Hare toured ten other industrial communities (including John Nolen's new town of Kingsport, Tennessee) for information on store counts, land values, transportation facilities, and similar practical matters before joining Kessler at Longview. Their work produced the basic scheme that still shapes the growth of the city. . . .

Like the Country Club neighborhoods . . . Longview was planned for the automobile. Main thoroughfares were given a 120-foot right-of-way with 60-foot roadways. Parkways represented the newest idea in moving automobiles rapidly through a city, as did a street layout that gave through traffic and industrial traffic bypasses around the business core and residential districts. Buses were used for public transit in place of streetcars whose trackage and routes hampered the free flow of Model Ts.

The influence of Kessler was probably apparent in the integrated park system of the new city. The six-acre civic center provided both a physical and symbolic focal point, as well as a buffer between the business and residential zones. Dredging turned swampy Fowler's Slough into the interconnected pools of Lake Sacajawea. The two million cubic yards of earth pumped out of the slough were used to fill and grade residential districts. West of the townsite, 400-foot Mount Solo was preserved as regional open space with hiking and riding trails.

Also like Nichols' developments, Longview was "zoned" by the use of restrictive covenants in subdivision dedications and deeds. Land-use zoning as a popular tool for public regulation of development was an innovation that dated only from the adoption of a comprehensive zoning code in New York in 1916. In new developments that did not yet have a municipal government, private use of restrictive covenants allowed a developer to guarantee the same stability in the pattern of land uses. In addition, the state of Washington had not yet adopted legislation to allow smaller municipalities to zone themselves. The planners, therefore, divided Longview into a number of distinct districts with different limitations on the size, value, type, and use of all buildings within the district. There was a retail district, a wholesale district, a light industrial district, a small apartment district west of the civic center, an expensive "West Side" neighborhood (where houses had to have a minimum value of $3,000), the more modest St. Helens neighborhood (minimum $1,000), the working-class Highlands neighborhood near the mill, and the Olympic neighborhood west of Lake Sacajawea (where the minimum price of houses dropped with distance from the lake). The Longview Company reserved the right of approval for house styles, fences, and grading. The restrictions ran for 20 years (to 1943 or 1944) with provision for automatic extension.

Development of the central business district was also carefully managed, with Commerce Street designated as the main business thoroughfare. As the first major business structure, the company-oriented Columbia River Mercantile anchored the downtown. Architects carefully designed other business buildings to provide retail space on the first floor, office space on the second floor for Commerce Street and corner properties, and high-class apartments on the second floor along the secondary business streets. Buildings that were surfaced with gleaming terra cotta cost a few hundred dollars extra to erect but returned several thousand more on resale.

The final characteristic that links Longview to the Nichols approach is its ambitious scale. With the approval of R. A. Long, Kessler and Hare designed a major city rather than a mill town. The amount of residential land and the size of the commercial district were scaled for a community of approximately 50,000 people. The plan gave Longview a framework to grow into. Rather than spreading outward from a single center, with resulting inefficiency and waste from a continual building and rebuilding of close-in districts, Longview grew "inward" or "together" from its several different nuclei. A map of 1926 shows seven distinct clusters of development separated by open land–retail district, mill, railroad district, St. Helens, West Side, Olympic, and Columbia Valley Gardens neighborhoods. As the city neared its goal of 50,000 population by 1930, the districts were

expected to fill out and touch one another and complete the city plan.

Longview was not a utopia intended to promise a distinct way of life for a select circle of believers. Nor was it a company town where the major employer retained direct control over the lives of employees as landlord, storekeeper, and police force. Instead, Longview was squarely within the American mainstream as an up-to-date example of the "open community." It was built for growth and intended to accommodate all comers who could pay the asking price, either for residential property or for industrial sites. As R. A. Long put it in 1928 in his address at the dedication of Long High School, it was "a city open to all—a city free from the domination of any interests—a city where all legitimate entrepreneurs would be welcome—a city designed along the most modern lines—a city that would profit by the mistakes of other cities—a city that would be clean and beautiful."

In practical terms, Long's ambitions translated into two more specific goals. First, the town was intended to support the company by attracting high quality, family-oriented workers. The aim was the same as in Lowell, Massachusetts, in the 1830s or Pullman, Illinois, in the 1880s, but without the undemocratic element of social control and compulsion. Second, the town was to generate money as a real estate development. The steps taken by the company in the early 1920s—building the 200-room Hotel Monticello as one of the first major structures, helping to start up a newspaper, promoting the town through advertising—were the same as those taken by city boosters in Chicago or Denver two and three generations earlier. To meet these goals, Longview had to match the values of the American middle class in the 1920s—businesslike, pleasant, and socially conservative.

The development of Longview was in the hands of the Long-Bell Company and its employees. Grading for the first streets started in August 1922. Wesley Vandercook supervised the construction of 14 miles of dikes to protect the low-lying site from floods. Many of the construction workers were housed in temporary two-room buildings brought in on skids. The first permanent housing was also built close to the mills to meet the needs of workmen, including both a dormitory and 250 small bungalows in the St. Helens and Highlands districts that were financed by the Longview Company. The first lot sold in February 1923, and dedication ceremonies for the town took place on July 23 when the hotel opened for business. . . .

The continued promotion of the town was very much R. A. Long's personal enterprise. . . . [He] used his own influence and money to support public amenities. Over several years in the late 1920s, he paid directly for landscaping Broadway and Lake Sacajawea, for street trees, the public library, and the city high school. Accounts estimate that he put roughly $1 million of his personal funds directly into the city.

Community development followed a pattern much like that in other American cities in the 1920s. Longview was incorporated as a municipality in February 1924, with its residents assuming responsibility for the standard range of city services. When the town staged its Pageant of Progress July 31 through August 2, 1924, to celebrate "the opening of the giant manufacturing plant of the Long Bell Lumber Company . . . and the first anniversary of the new city," the order of march for the parade gave some idea of the evolution of the community. There were floats or decorated automobiles from merchants, auto dealers, banks, civic clubs, and fraternal and social organizations.

The Longview Chamber of Commerce vigorously promoted the continued growth of the city. Its efforts at industrial recruitment supplemented those of the company, and it added a special interest in tourism. Indeed, Longview in the 1920s was proclaimed a tourist mecca of the Northwest, midway between majestic Mount Rainer and Mount St. Helens and the grandeur of the Pacific Ocean. Completion of the bridge across the Columbia in 1930 placed the city on the direct route from Puget Sound to Portland or the Oregon coast.

An exception to Longview as an ideal community was its casual institutionalization of racism. As in most other cities of the 1920s, Longview's restrictive covenants limited residence to "persons of the white race." The only omission was several blocks east of the business district, half a mile from other residential areas.

We can test both the achievements and problems of the mid-1920s with contrasting descriptions by visiting journalists. Writing in *Forbes* in 1924, Agnes Laut offered a rave review. Expecting to visit a frantic and slightly sleazy boom town, she found herself instead in something closer to an ideal. She stressed Longview as an experiment in enlightened self-interest and praised the boulevarded, flowered, and tree-lined Broadway as the rival of Fifth Avenue or Riverside Drive in New York for beauty and magnificence. Geddes Smith, in contrast, looked at the same magnificent distances with considerable skepticism. Writing in *The Survey* in 1927, he noted the survival of the "temporary" worker housing of Skidville and other low-quality housing as an anomalous note in a model city. He found the city hard to find among the empty blocks around the railroad station and civic center. . . .

Like much of the rest of the United States, Longview took a long time-out during the Great Depression. With the city's population passing 10,000 at the end of the 1920s (far short of the original 30,000 goal), local boosters confidently predicted a population of more than 20,000 by 1940. In point of fact, the total was only 12,385. The Long-Bell Company, which had put $9 million into the townsite and more than $40 million into its mills, drainage, and logging operations during the booming 1920s, was forced into retrenchment and reorganization by the Depression. It returned to profitability only in the 1950s (a few years before the merger into International Paper). Robert A. Long died in 1935.

The depression years also brought an additional phase in Longview's career as an experiment of city planning. One of the curious products of the New Deal was the "subsistence homesteads" program, established in 1933 by the National Industrial Recovery Act "to provide for aiding in the redistribution of the overbalance of population in industrial centers." The program combined a depression-era concern with urban unemployment, in the fervent belief in the moral superiority of going "back to the land." During 1934 and 1935, the Subsistence Homesteads Division in the Department of the Interior began to build several thousand homes in four types of communities: (1) for stranded industrial workers, (2) for farming combined with part-time decentralized industry, (3) for stranded farm populations, and (4) for industrial workers on the edge of existing industrial sites (farmettes).

Longview was chosen as the site for a community of the last type. The federal government paid the Longview Company $28,500 for 141 acres in the Columbia Valley Gardens area, a district on the west edge of the city that the original plan had set aside for precisely such semi-subsistence housing. The Subsistence Homesteads Division (later subsumed under the Resettlement Administra-

tion and Farm Security Administration) built 60 houses of four, five, or six rooms on approximately two acres each. A garage and an outbuilding on skids were also provided with the intention that occupants keep a cow and chickens as well as gardens. The initial families were selected from 450 applications and moved in on October 27, 1935. All of them were local residents with employment in the Longview/Kelso area. Most were in debt or had no assets and earned an average annual salary of $1,059.

Members of the new community formed a nonprofit association and bought the project from the federal government for $174,900 to be paid over 40 years. The members in turn bought their homesteads from the association over the same time period. Compared to many of the projects elsewhere around the United States, the Longview homesteads were built with no local opposition and few problems. Rex Willard, regional director of the Resettlement Administration, commented that Longview was one of the best models for the nation, as "ideal laboratory social test for this type of thing in the entire United States."

Not until a new Northwest resource boom arrived with hydroelectric power and war production around 1940 did Longview begin to grow. The construction of a Reynolds Metals Company aluminum plant in 1941 helped to diversify the town's economy. War production demands also boosted the wood products industry. When the city celebrated its 25th anniversary in 1949 (one year late because of the Columbia River floods of 1948), the population had reached 20,000, to be followed by slower but steady growth in ensuing decades.

Perhaps in reaction to the self-satisfaction of its developers, recent architectural and design critics have tended to be somewhat negative in their evaluation of Longview.

David Streatfield of the University of Washington commented on the town's "old-fashioned" formality of design as a relic of an earlier era of planning thought. Architectural historian Roger Montgomery called it both "overdesigned and under developed." Steve Dotterrer agreed that the plan provided amenities for Longview residents but that it lacked an understanding of the social and economic forces that were to push the city in directions unforeseen and unaccommodated by the plan.

To an outside observer, however, it appears that Longview has entered the last decade of the century with its original plan largely intact and functional. Population within the city reached 23,349 by 1960, 28,373 by 1970, and 31,052 by 1980, with another 9,830 in the adjacent urbanized area west of the Cowlitz River and 14,080 in Kelso and its environs east of the Cowlitz. The urbanized area has thus reached the population total anticipated by Longview's builders, but finds it spread over unanticipated distances by multi-automobile households.

This postwar population growth has been adequate to support housing that has filled most of the gaps that so bothered Geddes Smith. Longview's greatest design disappointment is shared with cities like Washington and Cincinnati that are 20 or 50 times its size, for the decline of rail travel and the demolition of the depot in the 1960s left Broadway as a ceremonial street without a ceremonial function.

Automobile-oriented strip development has certainly altered the balance of retail activities but has not destroyed the proto-urban core. In the center of the city, however, recent reinvestment has brought some new life to the business district. R. A. Long Park (Jefferson Square) remains a focal point for city-wide or area-wide civic institutions such as the library, city hall, and community college. The old neighborhoods, especially West Side and St. Helens, retain their original identities and still support something like the community that R. A. Long hoped for.

Historical Access to the Hanford Record
Problems in Investigating the Past
by Michele A. Stenehjem

The study in which I have been engaged is an environmental history of the Hanford Nuclear Reservation, 1945-1960, with a focus on the public policy questions that have been raised by the "coming to light" of the evidence in the "Hanford Historical Documents" in the last three and a half years. . . .

The very heart of my purpose in pursuing this research is to examine and raise debate about the ways in which public policy decisions about atomic (or nuclear) matters are made in the United States. To me, the study of Hanford's history raises fundamental questions about American democracy. Chief among these questions is that of secrecy and national security versus the individual's right to have access to basic health and safety data in order to make his or her own choice—as an individual or as the head of a family—about what levels of risk to choose to accept or to move away from. . . . In other words, how was the decision made and who had the authority in this democracy to choose not to inform atomic workers . . . in 1949, for example, that an experiment . . . has released 5,500 curies of radioiodine (I-131) . . . in a huge cloud surrounding the Tri-Cities, knowing that I-131 concentrates in the thyroid—especially the thyroids of children, infants, and fetuses—and that it can be inhaled directly or ingested through the milk of cows and goats that eat forage vegetation on which the radioiodine has settled? Or, for example, how was the policy decision made in August and September 1954 not to inform farmers working the wheat harvest in northern Franklin County, Washington, that an acci-

dental release of radiourthenium (Ru103 and Ru106) had occurred, knowing that crops would proceed to market and that particles adhering to the crops and the soil would remain radioactive for a year? How is it that we developed in this country a technology so new, so secret, so little understood by the public, so technical, so unregulated, that incidents of these types could and did occur and nowhere did any law or policy require that the public be informed?

Other salient public policy questions raised by the study of the history of Hanford are as follows:

—What are the limits of federal authority?

—What is the role of local and state governments? How informed should they be and how much should they participate in policy decisions regarding federal activities within their borders and jurisdictions?

—How, in this nation, do we regulate or supervise new technologies? What happens to scientific peer review when all of the pertinent data from an emerging science are classified?

—Should there be federal liability for past damages done to civilians or military personnel who were exposed to radioactivity?

—Is a population which lives near a major atomic defense production site actually living in a combat zone?

—If, in the 1940s and 1950s, the Hanford reservation needed to pollute in order to produce, should the government have bought up huge buffer zones around this installation; prohibited farming, ranching, hunting, fishing, and recreational water use; and brought in all food by truck and train? Who should have made that decision?

—Finally, how and by whom are decisions made in the United States about what is "best" for all of us? . . .

Access to the Hanford record is unquestionably difficult, even when documents are not officially classified. Many key reports are still classified, and Freedom of Information Act requests are denied on the basis that if you know how much radiophosphorus was in the tissues of Columbia River whitefish in 1957, for example, you may be able to deduce or extrapolate . . . the production levels of the reactors lining the river at that time! The production and power levels of the reactors, even as far back as 1944, still are classified as secret. Revealing those figures, I have been told by the Department of Ecology as recently as January 1989, "could reasonably be expected to cause damage to the national security."

In terms of unclassified information, the Hanford Historical Documents themselves, in their entirety, are available at only one public location, the DOE Public Reading Room in Richland. . . .

To begin to grasp the attitudes which prevail at the DOE in Richland today, one important factor to consider is the tradition of seclusion and secrecy in which the whole Hanford endeavor has been carried out ever since its inception. The very location of the Hanford Reservation was chosen, in part, because it was remote and isolated. Safety concerns governed this decision. We learn from the records of the Manhattan Engineer District, available at the National Archives, that by late 1942, as the basic atomic and chemical experimentation work which eventually led to plutonium manufacture was being developed, the principal scientists involved in the Manhattan Project—scientists such as J. Robert Oppenheimer and Enrico

Fermi—became "duly impressed by the evidence of intense radioactivity in the separation process." This fact . . . subsequently contributed to the Military Policy Committee's decision in December to shift the plutonium production plant from" its planned location in Clinton, Tennessee, to a more "remote" location. When asked to take on the job of constructing the Hanford complex and begin the manufacture of weapons-grade plutonium, Walter S. Carpenter, the president of DuPont Corporation at that time, insisted that "due to the unknown an unanticipated hazards" of the process the plants be located outside of the populated East Coast corridor.

After the construction of Hanford in early 1943, the endeavor was kept so secret that even the Joint Chiefs of Staff were not told about it. The State Department was not informed until shortly before the pivotal Yalta Conference held among the top leaders of the allied nations in February 1945. Congressional representatives and senators, including Harry Truman, who wanted to investigate the secret army construction project during World War II, were contacted individually by Secretary of War Henry Stimson and told not to proceed with their investigations. Even after Truman was elected vice-president in November 1944, he was not informed about the Hanford project; in fact, he was not told until President Franklin D. Roosevelt died on April 12, 1945. Likewise, potential investigations of the secret endeavor by the American Federation of Labor and by several major newspapers were called off as the result of personal interventions by Secretary Stimson. Similarly, state and local selective service boards, courts, and civic leaders were kept in the dark, as were railroad inspectors from the Bureau of Explosives and stockholders of the companies and subcontractors involved in constructing Hanford's equipment and plants.

Everything about the Hanford enterprise was listed as coming within the restricted clauses in the wartime Code of Fair Practices. Even the amounts of beer and food consumed by the construction workers on the huge site were classified, so that enemy agents could not guess the scope of the project by the size of the work force. Newspaper editors throughout the Northwest were contacted in 1943 by Manhattan Project officials and asked to "cooperate . . . by not asking questions . . . or speculating in print" about the vast and mysterious structures being erected in the south-central Washington desert. In 1944, Lieutenant Milton Cydell, a former *Seattle Times* reporter, was recruited by General Leslie Groves, head of the Manhattan Project, briefed confidentially, and assigned to travel throughout the United States, meeting with editors to quell rumors and stories about the project.

The purposes of the Hanford endeavor were also kept secret from most of the engineers and all of the construction and support personnel who worked there. The wife of Franklin Matthias, the army colonel in command at Hanford during World War II, recalled that, even among the few high-level officials who did understand the plant's mission, the "famous HEW [Hanford Engineering Works] line . . . was 'I can't tell you' . . . and 'don't say anything to anyone.'" Another wartime wife recounted: "At first we housewives had an almost overpowering curiosity, which was soon replaced by complete indifference to the whole thing. . . . You soon learned to `see no rumor, speak no rumor, hear no rumor.'" A DuPont production manager at Hanford has told me that "we were forbidden to keep diaries or private notes. When we left the job, all our files nd working papers were left behind."

Recruiting firms scouring the country for manpower for the badly understaffed project were told to be vague as to location and job description. Once on site, work was kept compartmentalized and construction drawings "were broken down to disclose as little as possible." "Termination interviews" conducted by Hanford's placement office revealed that lack of knowledge about the work they were doing engendered so much frustration among some employees that it caused them to quit. Likewise, a chemist who went to work for the Health Instruments Division (the environmental monitoring section) at Hanford during its earliest years emphasized the highly secretive manner in which all duties on the project were carried out. He told me about his experiences when he was assigned to work with Hanford's chief health physicist, Dr. Herbert Parker. Parker called him in and said, "Never use the words uranium or plutonium here." Uranium was called "base metal," and plutonium was called "product." There were many other code words, he recalled.

After the atomic bombs were dropped on Hiroshima and Nagasaki, Japan, in August 1945, newspaper and radio reporters descended in a swarm on Richland, but they didn't learn much. Manhattan Project chief Groves authorized for the press a limited tour outside of the production area fences of the Hanford site, and a basic explanation of atomic theory was issued in a special government document entitled "The Smyth Report." Groves prohibited any "discussion of process, production, or the employment of the Atomic Bomb."

During the ensuing ten years, the Hanford Reservation underwent three major expansions. Throughout the Cold War, silence and secrecy continued as a way of life in Richland, a town where people simply never talked about their work. Another early Hanford chemist told me, "The town and plant were

ruled authoritatively by the company. . . .
Secrecy prevailed. It was not discrete [*sic*] to
speak of what was going on—even if one
knew legally or guessed what was happen-
ing. The indiscrete [*sic*] were shipped out of
town."

Recently, I organized a round-table discussion in Richland among several veterans
of "Camp Hanford" and anti-aircraft battal-
ions that protected the weapons production
facilities at Hanford from 1950 to 1960. This
was a *domestic* military base, operating in
peacetime. The men told me how they were
assigned to anti-aircraft duty "out West" and
were sent from Fort Bliss, Texas, where they
had trained, to Fort Lewis, near Tacoma,
Washington. From Fort Lewis they were con-
veyed to Hanford, still without being told
anything about where they were going or
why. These men found me very amusing and
roared with laughter when I asked, "Well,
then, when you got to Hanford, were you
given a tour or briefed?" "No ma'am," they
answered, "the army told us nothing!" They
were driven out to forward bunkers amidst
the sand and sagebrush, where the 120mm
guns and Nike missiles were placed. On alert
every time an aircraft came near, still they
were told nothing. "Well," I asked them,
"what did your officers say when you asked
them questions about the mission?" Again
they exploded with laughter. "Questions!"
they said, "Are you crazy? We never questioned anything the army told us to do!" The
two officers present in my group around the
table merely scowled. . . .

When incidents of gross environmental
contamination occurred, Hanford's managers, chief health physicist Parker, and Atomic
Energy Commission officials would exchange a flurry of correspondence about how
to handle "the public relations problem." In
the case of the 1954 radiouthenium releases,
Herbert Parker stated in an internal memo:

"Nothing is to be gained by informing the
public. . . . Not all the residents will be as
relaxed as the one who recently was quoted
as saying, 'Living in Richland is ideal because we breathe only tested air.' . . . The
[public] relations problem will be a severe
one."

From 1954 through 1966, an ongoing debate was conducted among the few scientists
and officials who did have access to the
classified data concerning radioactivity levels in Columbia River fish. The questions of
possibly closing popular sport fishing areas
near the Hanford Reach of the river came up
for discussion repeatedly. By 1960, radioactive contamination levels in Columbia River
whitefish muscle tissues were so high that
the consumption of just one pound of whitefish flesh per week could bring an adult
human to the maximum permissible concentration level for radiophosphorus (P32). The
situation for local duck flesh was the same.
Yet, Hanford chief health physicist Parker
repeatedly advised that closing public fishing and hunting would frighten the public
and damage Hanford's public reputation.
"The possibility of damage exists," he stated
in an internal document reviewing radioactive pollution in the Columbia River. However, he believed that the conceivable hazards were "overshadowed by the public relations effect. . . . The relations situation is
always potentially dangerous, and it will be
severely taxed if and when actual restrictions . . . on sport fishing are recommended."

In 1957, Hanford scientists completed a
secret report on the potential problems asso-
ciated with opening the Hanford Reach to
commercial barge navigation. Barge crew-
men, they acknowledged, could be at risk
from drinking raw river water along the
way. Should they recommend the issuance
of orders restricting water use for drinking
purposes? Their secret report concluded that

such restrictions would cause "little inconvenience....However, public relations might suffer from such restrictions." Clearly, this was not a group of decision-makers that placed a high value on openness.

Ironically, in July 1950 the Atomic Energy Commission issued a specific promise of open disclosure in a public report to Congress. "Basic science should be free," stated the AEC, "except where it is directly related to weapons." At that time, the commission pledged that it would maintain a sunshine policy on all data and knowledge which did not pertain to "weapons information, including design, production and stockpiles . . . the use of atomic energy for industrial purposes . . . or [any facts which would] help the atomic energy program of a potential enemy." Did these criteria include the classification of thousands of pages of environmental monitoring reports? One might think not, but in actual practice the answer is yes. The AEC and officials of Hanford's operating contractor, the General Electric Corporation (GE), combined this pledge of open disclosure with continual, repeated public assistance reassurances that the operations at Hanford were totally safe, well-controlled, and harmless. As a result, few, if anyone, among the public doubted that the Columbia Basin was safe.

In February 1986, the first 19,000 pages of Hanford Historical Documents were released. Less than two months later, in mid-April 1986, the world's worst nuclear accident (of which we are aware) occurred at Chernobyl in the Soviet Union. In the flurry of investigations which followed, it came to the attention of the press and the public that the graphite containment system on the Soviet reactors was the same as the safety system of the N-reactor, the last large-reduction reactor operating on the Hanford site. A panel of safety experts known as the Roddis Panel, . . . headed by nuclear utility expert Louis H. Roddis, was formed by U.S. Energy Secretary John S. Herrington. This group was directed to examine the safety systems on N-reactor. Later in 1986, the Roddis Panel recommended the shutdown of this reactor in order that safety modifications could be installed. N-reactor did shut down in January 1987, and it has never restarted. In February 1988, the U.S. DOE placed this unit on "cold standby," precipitating an economic crisis in the Tri-Cities. . . .

[Also in 1986,] . . . the Washington State Department of Social and Health Services called in an M.D./epidemiologist from the federal Centers for Disease Control in Atlanta, Georgia, and asked him to compute a preliminary, possible dose range to which the population of the Columbia Basin may have been exposed in the 1940s and 1950s. Together with Oregon and the Indian Health Service, Washington state also empaneled the Hanford Health Effects Review Panel, a group of experts asked to review and comment upon the radiation doses and releases which were disclosed in the Hanford Historical Documents. In October 1987, after more than a year of study, this panel issued its recommendations. Dr. A. James Ruttenber, panel member, stated that "the amounts of radiation released from Hanford between 1944 and 1955 add up to the largest public exposure from any U.S. nuclear facility in the atomic era." Among other things, the panel called for two large studies to be carried out.

Now, after much negotiation, disagreement, posturing, and several false starts, the two studies have begun. The first one, known as the Hanford Dose Reconstruction Project, is funded by the DOE and carried out by the Battelle Pacific Northwest Laboratories in Richland. . . . The aim of the study is to establish statistical bands of probability for radioactive emissions. . . .

The other study . . . is funded by Congress and carried out by the federal Centers for Disease Control. . . . This project is a health effects study, the aim of which in its first and current phase is to look at the incidence of thyroid disease in selected locations in eastern Washington. Thyroid disorders, especially hypothyroidism, thyroid nodules, and thyroid cancer, are largely radiogenic in nature and can be traced to the presence of I-131 in the air and food chain. . . .

. . . The very presence of outside experts and the highly visible position of Hanford as the first defense weapons production facility to be studied in such detail has seemed to make the DOE feel a sense of accountability. At this time, the DOE seems to realize that its decisions and policies are and will continue to be subject to credible, fair, scientific peer review. In this case, I see historians playing one of their most valuable roles—that of directly and visibly helping to shape present policy and make our democratic system of checks and balances, of fairness, honesty, and dignity and value of each member of the public, stand stronger and work better. . . .

Recommended Readings

Allen, John Eliot, and Marjorie Burns. *Cataclysms on the Columbia*. Portland, Oregon: Timber Press, 1986.

———. *The Magnificent Gateway*. Forest Grove, Oregon: Timber Press, 1979.

Balch, Frederic Homer. *The Bridge of the Gods*. Portland, Oregon: Binfords & Mort, 1965.

Binns, Archie. *You Rolling River*. New York: Ballantine Books, 1947.

Bullard, Oral. *Crisis on the Columbia*. Portland, Oregon: Touchstone Press, 1968.

Davis, H. L. *The Distant Music*. Sausalito, California: Comstock, 1957.

Holbrook, Stewart. *The Columbia*. New York: Rinehart and Co., 1956.

Hunn, Eugene S. *Nch'i-Wana, "The Big River": Mid-Columbia Indians and Their Land*. Seattle: University of Washington Press, 1990.

Hussey, John A. *The History of Fort Vancouver and Its Physical Structure*. Tacoma: Washington State Historical Society, 1957.

Jones, Nard. *Swift Flows the River*. New York: Dodd, Mead & Company, 1940.

Lesley, Craig. *River Song*. Boston: Houghton Mifflin Company, 1989.

McClelland, John, Jr. *R. A. Long's Planned City: The Story of Longview*. Rev. ed. Longview, Washington: Longview Publishing Company, 1976.

Mills, Randall. *Stern-Wheelers up Columbia: A Century of Steamboating in the Oregon Country*. 1947. Reprint. Lincoln: University of Nebraska Press, 1977.

Morgan, Murray. *The Columbia*. Seattle: Superior Publishing Company, 1949.

———. *The Dam*. New York: Viking Press, 1954.

Moulton, Gary E., ed. *Journals of the Lewis and Clark Expedition*. 7 vols. [to date] Lincoln: University of Nebraska Press, 1991.

Netboy, Anthony. *The Columbia River Salmon and Steelhead Trout: Their Fight for Survival*. Seattle: University of Washington Press, 1980.

Neuberger, Richard L. *Our Promised Land*. Moscow: University of Idaho Press, 1966.

Nokes, J. Richard. *Columbia's River: The Voyages of Robert Gray, 1787-1793*. Tacoma: Washington State Historical Society, 1991.

Pomeroy, Earl. *The Pacific Slope: A History of California, Oregon, Washington, Idaho, Utah, and Nevada*. New York: Knopf, 1965.

Relander, Click. *Dreamers and Drummers*. Seattle: Pacific Northwest National Parks and Forests Association, 1986.

Ronda, James P. *Astoria and Empire*. Lincoln: University of Nebraska Press, 1990.

———. *Lewis and Clark Among the Indians*. Lincoln: University of Nebraska Press, 1984.

Ross, Alexander. *Adventures of the First Settlers on the Oregon or Columbia River, 1810-1813*. Lincoln: University of Nebraska Press, 1986.

Ruby, Robert H., and John A. Brown. *The Chinook Indians: Traders of the Lower Columbia*. Norman: University of Oklahoma Press, 1976.

Seufert, Francis. *Wheels of Fortune*. Portland: Oregon Historical Society, 1980.

Strong, Emory. *Stone Age on the Columbia River*. Portland, Oregon: Binfords & Mort, 1959.

Van Arsdol, Ted. *Hanford, the Big Secret*. Richland, Washington: Columbia Basin News, 1959.

Willingham, William. *Army Engineers and the Development of Oregon*. Portland, Oregon: U.S. Army Engineer District, 1983.

Wright, Robin K., ed. *A Time of Gathering: Native Heritage in Washington State*. Seattle: University of Washington Press, 1991.

Steamboat passing the palisades at Cape Horn on the Columbia River
(Oregon Historical Society, CN004455)